YORK FILM NOTES

Easy Rider

Director
Dennis Hopper

Note by Iain Colley

Longman

Y York Press

For my sons, and in memory of their mother

York Press
322 Old Brompton Road, London SW5 9JH

Pearson Education Limited
Edinburgh Gate, Harlow, Essex CM20 2JE, United Kingdom
Associated companies, branches and representatives throughout
the world

All stills are reproduced by courtesy of Columbia Pictures and are
© Columbia Pictures
Screenplay extracts in York Film Notes: *Easy Rider* by Iain Colley are printed
by courtesy of Columbia Pictures and are © Columbia Pictures

Stills obtained from Huntley Picture Library

First published 2000

ISBN 0-582-43195-6

Designed by Vicki Pacey
Phototypeset by Gem Graphics, Trenance, Mawgan Porth, Cornwall
Colour reproduction and film output by Spectrum Colour
Printed in Great Britain by Henry Ling Limited, Dorchester, Dorset

contents

It is not a man's duty, as a matter
  of course, to devote himself to the
eradication of any, even the most
  enormous wrong; he may still
properly have other concerns to
  engage him; but it is his duty, at
least, to wash his hands of it, and,
  if he gives it no thought longer,
not to give it practically his support.

H. D. Thoreau, 'Civil Disobedience'

Freedom's just another word
  for nothing left to lose.

Kris Kristofferson, 'Me and Bobby McGee'

author of this note Dr Iain Colley is a freelance writer
and lecturer based in Lancaster. A student at the University of Sussex in
the late 1960s, he has taught American Literature, Film Studies and
Writing Studies at a number of institutions. His fiction and verse have
appeared in Stand, The Affectionate Punch, New Poetry, Pulse Fiction and
Northern Stories among other publications.

EASY RIDER

background

Thirty years ago, when *Easy Rider* was first released, it would have seemed anomalous to consider it as an object of serious study. Film Studies had begun, and their pioneers were arming for the struggle, but had still a long way to go before they would be a legitimate discipline. 'Hollywood' was hardly an educated person's concern, other than as a source of light entertainment. To be serious about art meant feeling superior to Hollywood; art worth taking seriously mainly meant English Literature.

But in the most unstable of situations – 1968 had been a year of revolution across the world – change was inevitable. Dynamic new social forces, such as second-wave feminism and the gay liberation movement, would become permanent presences. On the educational front, perspectives broadened until everything – including the trivial and the taboo – became available for study. Film and Media Studies took their place in the curriculum, and the rebellious students of the 1960s grew up to be the church elders of the new disciplines. Meantime *Easy Rider* recirculates as a movie which owes much – its original success and its current status – to the volatile passions of the late 1960s.

trailer

Easy Rider is a film that won't go away. It has become identified with that mythical decade 'The Sixties' (most histories of the USA in the 1960s – not of American cinema alone – mention it). There are those, however, who damn it as an irresponsible contribution to that myth. The story concerns two not-so-beautiful losers, rootless romantic failures. In an age where smooth success is the approved goal, it may look quaintly archaic. More than most films, it is a movie of its time. And thirty years of history have not abolished its meanings, only added to them.

To say that a film lasts is one way of describing a classic. *Easy Rider* will never be a revered classic of film art on the level of *Battleship Potemkin* or

Citizen Kane. But it is much more than a dated curiosity, or a nostalgic trip. First of all, it is exciting, a fast hour and a half. Little happens, but at great speed, and the tale is driven by a tremendous anthology of rock songs. Visually, it shows off the scope and variety of the American landscape as only cinema can. It is also a far from humourless film, with a surprisingly comic distance, often overlooked, on its heroes.

Billy and Wyatt are superheroes only in their dreams. They are not brave or noble. They're not even very intelligent or emotionally expressive. But for all their purposeless drift and their sad end, they are not contemptible. They stand for something which neither they nor the movie can fully articulate, which belongs to history. *Easy Rider* was shot in 1968, the peak year of the 1960s (see Contexts: 1968). Though it deliberately avoids precise contemporary references, it is saturated in the hot blend of feelings that dominated America then.

It is probably no accident that a movie with scant intellectual depth is so emotionally powerful. The social debates of 1969 were vigorous and hectic, not cool position papers. High on the list of youth demands were imagination, sensory pleasure and feeling. Like sex, drugs and rock 'n' roll? Yes, among other things. The youth of the 1960s willed their right to pleasure into being against the sneering disapproval of an alarmed establishment.

No analysis can take place without considering the historical dimension of a film. This has two poles, then and now, with thirty years of calamitous change in between. What I see now in *Easy Rider* is an engrossing movie experience; a familiar love-hate relationship with America; some self-conscious silliness; and a penumbra of values that still have relevance. *Easy Rider* is no fossilised Sixties' relic, but to understand this adequately entails first of all viewing it in its original context.

Films are made by production companies. They are also made by audiences, reviewers and critics. Reference books date films according to the year of their release, not of their shooting schedule, because that is when the public gets to see them. Until then a film may as well be an unpublished book. And what happens when films are received is full of mysteries (though see Contexts: Audiences).

cinema audiences have minds of their own

Hollywood has mostly worked to popular genres: musicals, comedies, romantic dramas, thrillers, Westerns, SF and so forth. At the heart of this policy is the belief that the public will come back for more of what it likes. There must be some variation, but that usually is in the surface detail. Sadly for the box office, predicting audience taste is not an exact science. Many films lose money, despite having all the right ingredients. Making movies is more of a gamble than most businesses, because even the preview system cannot guarantee that the expensively made product will appeal to enough people to recover its costs. Cinema audiences have minds of their own.

Between the studios and the public stand the reviewers and critics, some serious, some lightweight. Though not universally respected, they offer a range of information and critical judgements on the latest releases. They can help shape opinion and in turn exert some influence on the success or failure of a film, though film-goers have often ignored them and voted with their feet. Further, reviewers' assumptions about what constitutes a good or bad film may allow us to glimpse the hidden agendas (see Contexts: Ideology) of a society and its processes of cultural production.

Easy Rider was implicitly labelled an art movie when it was picked as the official American entry at Cannes, where it carried off the prize for the best film by a new director. It also got two Oscar nominations (Best Original Screenplay; Best Supporting Actor – Jack Nicholson). And it wasn't too arty to worry the trade. *Variety* praised it as a movie for 'both youthful and selective audiences, with art chances promising'. While this reflected the showbiz industry rather than a critical analysis, its prediction was amply confirmed.

Boxoffice Movie Review shared *Variety's* confident prediction, and added 'it will be easy for many to misinterpret this "drug" store fantasy as one of those facile crucifixion tales about the "good guys" who must be destroyed by a corrupt and backward society, but there is a much more significant and frightening sub-surface here... '. It was concerned that the mythmaking aspects would conceal this significance, which it omitted to define (the touchy domestic politics of the Vietnam war, probably), but commended the picture as 'one of the major youth market attractions of the year'.

'lower case cinema'

Manny Farber, an idiosyncratic freelance critic, found it a 'lyrical, quirky film, pretty good' despite what he thought of as some 'draggy, romantic material'. He singled out Jack Nicholson for special praise. Farber's piece also warms to the visuals as 'beautiful'.

Vincent Canby in the *New York Times* was among the minority of dissenters, loftily calling *Easy Rider* 'lower case cinema'. The affected language points to a notion of art in which qualities such as high seriousness and profundity are primary: a less sensory appreciation of cinema than Farber's. And *Easy Rider* is nothing if not sensory.

They all saw the same film. Or did they? The trade's expectations of profit were correct. That fact can be objectively measured. But reviewers liked or disliked *Easy Rider* for a whole range of discordant reasons, according to their own aesthetic values. And aesthetic values are ultimately social, even political, values. Disagreement among the critics of *Easy Rider* mirrored the rifts in American society, in parallel with the movie itself. In this case, most of the reviewers shared some sort of recognition with the youth audience which *Easy Rider* addressed. They 'read' the film according to their predispositions. Just as the movie-going public does. (And just as I do.)

reading easy rider

Consider the abrupt opening of *Easy Rider*. The first sound is the revving of motorcycles; the bikes are initially off-screen. The first image is a static medium long shot – a master shot – of La Contenta Bar. No captions identify the location, but we understand it from the bar sign to be Mexico. Two bikers (Billy and Wyatt) ride into the frame. There follow cuts to the faces of onlookers, apparently Mexican labourers or field workers. Close-ups show lined work-worn features, resembling the documentary photo portraits of the Depression years in America. They seem interested, welcoming, friendly. The bar name's association with happiness is borne out by their cordial attitude. This is not the Mexico of so many Hollywood films, an insanitary hell of corruption, betrayal and death.

A more smartly dressed man (Jesús) comes out of the bar and warmly welcomes the two arrivals. He leads them, followed by the tracking camera, past a car dump. All dialogue is in Spanish, but their actions make clear that a drug deal is going down. There is a civilised feel to the ritual as they squat among auto parts to test the cocaine (though the drug is not named) and agree on its quality: 'pura vida' – pure life. Drugs and money are exchanged.

It is a warm, cross-cultural scene, making no attempt to milk shock value from the illegality of the drug deal. The viewer is invited to picture the back story that led up to it and it sets up questions and expectations about how it will proceed. At the end of this sequence noise intrudes. As Billy and Wyatt are being waved off, a jump cut reveals it to be the landing of planes at Los Angeles International Airport (again, we infer the exact location).

The bikers now have a white pickup and are selling what they bought in Mexico to a nervous, wealthy geek, The Connection (played by Phil Spector), complete with Rolls-Royce and spooky bodyguard/chauffeur. (There may be tongue-in-cheek allusions here to Spector's oddball image and to the high-tech, reclusive villains of Bond movies.) This time there is no special friendliness about the meeting, just a quick, efficient transaction. Nothing is said. Each party is satisfied. The Connection checks the goods while the chauffeur handles the money. Billy and Wyatt take off in their pickup. They cross a dusty landscape shot against the light, abstract and dreamlike, then a cut fills the screen with a blurred, abstract image. As focus is pulled, it becomes the shiny gas tank of a motorcycle.

At this point the first English words are heard:

> You know I smoked a lot of grass
> Oh Lord, I popped a lot of pills
> But I've never touched nothin'
> That my spirit could kill ...

The angry lyrics of Hoyt Axton's 'The Pusher' ('God damn the Pusher man'), performed by Steppenwolf, continue playing as the camera dwells admiringly on Wyatt's gleaming machine customised with the stars and stripes. He stuffs a plastic tube of money into the gas tank, settles his helmet over his head. The song ends as a further jump cut takes us to the start of their journey beside a stone ruin. It is symbolically marked by Wyatt's throwing his watch on the ground, rejecting clock time in favour 'a Chase-Caper-Road-Youth-Drug-Buddy film'

of personal time. As they head for the distant mountains, the credits appear.

Few film-goers now would find this pre-credit sequence disorienting. The visuals carry the story as effectively as the frames in a cartoon strip. What is happening is not hard to decipher. Foreign language dialogue and non-diegetic music are no longer novelties, nor is the choppy cutting. But in 1969 it was not the kind of movie normally released by Columbia, in Peter Biskind's words 'a stodgy, conservative studio almost totally out of step with the emerging counterculture'.

What *Easy Rider* brought to the screen was a sense of the thrill of movement and change, a freedom from conventional judgements, a relaxed attitude to the outlawed pleasures of drug use, heroes who were not driven by worldly success or the need for approval, the pounding rock songs that young people played at home (see Style: Music), and a cinematic style that disregarded the canons of the traditional well-fashioned, highly plotted feature film. It was a blast.

In fact *Easy Rider* is a film that can be approached from a number of perspectives: as a low-budget money-trap, a prototypical road movie, a Cannes prizewinner, a countercultural statement, a harbinger of the new Hollywood, a collection of art house clichés, a launch pad for Jack Nicholson's big-time career, a cult item, a tribute to mindbending chemicals, a one-off oddity from a past age, a 'classic'. Most apply. Peter Fonda originally saw it as a modern Western. James Monaco, in *American Film Now*, calls it 'a Chase-Caper-Road-Youth-Drug-Buddy film'. It sidesteps simple generic classification – in that respect, too, it looks forward to subsequent cinema.

Easy Rider is famous, iconic, but, despite its initial welcome by audiences, not always well regarded critically. Critical opinion in the hectic years since 1969 has often been unkind to it. Gilbert Adair's *Hollywood's Vietnam* views it as a movie 'undone by its own intrusive narcissism'. Leonard Quart and Albert Auster, in *American Film and Society since 1945*, find it 'inarticulate, shallow and pretentious when it comes to dealing with ideas'. Even to those who once shared the outlook of its two anti-heroes it can be a lingering embarrassment. Much of the stoned, 'groovy', near-moronic

Crossing the bridge,
and leaving behind
the mechanised culture
which its angular iron
girders represent, to go
'looking for America'

dialogue sounds dated (though not inaccurate) and at moments the camp-fire scenes look just that: camp. But an embarrassing movie is not a dead or insignificant movie. Quart and Auster balance their critique with the observation that 'it struck a powerful social and emotional chord' in the climate of the late 1960s.

There is no question that it captures and preserves some of the Zeitgeist. The years 1968–9 furnished the exceptional conditions under which it could be made and be a stunning 'sleeper'. Hollywood was in the process of change, of seeking new genres and new audiences after the dissolution of the old studio system. American society was being shaken by events that divided the nation (see Contexts: Political) and pitted the young and radical against their conservative parents' generation (the 'silent majority', as right-wing politicians tended to call it). Sex, drugs and rock 'n' roll were a slogan and a lifestyle. The shadow of the Vietnam war clouded the political landscape, though Hollywood dared not tackle it directly till much later. Students were challenging the old authoritarian structures of their universities. On the cultural front, it was a time for experimentation (see Contexts: Cultural & Cinematic).

Easy Rider certainly owed its success to the energy of change. It is not fully innovative, but it pointed the way to the New Hollywood, where the art film and the commercial movie were no longer so distinct from one another and fresh talent could make its mark. *Easy Rider* was an invigorating shock to many of its original audience, because it told its story from the viewpoint of two dropouts and drug-users without moralising about their lifestyle. It blew the old, tame 'youth picture', which always aimed to reconcile the generations, out of the water.

key players' biographies

Easy Rider's origins lay in a combination of a fruitful market opportunity, the desire of Peter Fonda and Dennis Hopper to make a personal film, adventurous backers (see Contexts: Industrial) and a volatile blend of talent. Fonda conceived the idea on a Canadian promotional tour in 1967, while gazing, stoned, at a publicity picture of himself and Bruce Dern in Roger Corman's 1966 biker movie, *The Wild Angels*. His instant vision was of 'two wounded heroes, searchers' setting out across the country together. Memories of Western screen heroes inspired him; his character's name recalls the legendary marshal Wyatt Earp, whom his father had played in John Ford's *My Darling Clementine* (1946).

When he contacted Dennis Hopper to share the idea, Hopper responded with supercharged enthusiasm. For additional know-how, they turned to Terry Southern, a 'gonzo' author and highly successful screenwriter, who agreed to write the screenplay for scale – ten weeks' work at $350 a week. Southern, in typical freaky manner, developed the script in pot-smoking, brainstorming sessions with the other two at his New York office, later allowing them to share the writing credit.

Dennis Hopper and Peter Fonda fell out during the making of *Easy Rider*. It is almost inevitable that creative collaborators will, but Hopper had a talent for falling out with everyone. Many thought of him as a violent, drug-crazed egomaniac. By all accounts, including his own, he acted like one on set, ranting and cursing at the crew from the first day of shooting. (It has also been suggested that Fonda privately took advantage of Terry Southern's withdrawal from the profit-sharing arrangement to make extra money for his own film company, though Southern has denied that he had points in *Easy Rider*.)

Some of the stress between them shows on screen, and helps the story by injecting tensions other than the central Us vs Them conflict. It underlines, among other things, that the counterculture which their characters represented was not a unified movement with a single agenda. Quarrels and differences abounded in the alternative, as in straight, society. Some 'freaks' were political, some not. Some wanted just to drop out, others were committed to pursuing new ideas.

The fictional Billy and Wyatt could be aligned with the former tendency, Hopper and Fonda with the latter. *Easy Rider* owes a lot to their idealistic belief that a 'true' youth film could be made. But they couldn't ignore the ways of Hollywood to get it made. And this they were equipped to do. Though not prominent figures, neither was a newcomer on the Hollywood scene. In fact they were not that young, Hopper born in 1936, Fonda four years later. Fonda was the scion of a Hollywood dynasty: Henry, his father, was a big star, nearly always in dignified liberal roles. His elder sister, Jane, had already started an acting career that led her to major parts and much notoriety. Once politicised, she became 'Hanoi Jane', a hate-object for the right. Peter was the family problem child, moody and eclipsed by his father's fame. He led a troubled youth. He had been badly affected by the suicide of his mother, Frances, after his parents' marriage had failed, and was often at war with his father.

He was already an actor of some experience, having played stage and television parts and appeared in several movies, including two for Roger Corman, who was associated with American International Pictures (AIP). But he was still a marginal figure, and felt frustrated with the low profile of his career to date. Making *Easy Rider* would be a way of securing his own identity in the public eye, out of Henry's shadow, though he fails to project charisma. He had also begun trying out drugs and generally identifying himself with the movement of rebellious youth. His 'alternative' image had been aired in both *The Wild Angels* and *The Trip* (1967), the latter a semidocumentary film that, as Corman planned it, was open-minded about the LSD experience.

Hopper came from Dodge City, famous in Western lore, though his family moved to southern California when he was a child. He had been appearing in movies since 1955, but typically he had blighted his film career by what studios and directors saw as an attitude problem. As a result, much of his work during the early 1960s had been in television.

His image was already that of a nonconformist. One of his earliest film roles cast him as a member of the high school gang tormenting James Dean in *Rebel Without a Cause* (1955). He had found in Dean a kindred spirit and role model. In Dean's last film, *Giant* (1955), Hopper played the rancher's son who married a Mexican wife against Anglo prejudice. It was a clean-cut, sympathetic part and he was much less striking in it than in the later characterisations that stamped him as a heavy, a misfit or a weirdo. Immediately before *Easy Rider* he had appeared in the John Wayne vehicle *True Grit* and (uncredited, as himself) in the Monkees' movie *Head* as well as *The Trip*.

Hopper certainly had a reputation as a 'head', and according to Fonda his first instinct when he heard of the *Easy Rider* project was to insist that Billy and Wyatt should be cocaine dealers (cocaine was not then the drug of choice, as it became in the 1980s).

Both men were young and hip enough to be in tune with the potential audience for a film like *Easy Rider*, and they had the industry connections. However, neither had taken executive responsibility for shooting a movie, though Hopper had directed some of the second-unit filming for *The Trip*. This helped convince Fonda of his ability. They were close to Hollywood, but not completely of Hollywood, and novices as regards the production and direction of a feature film. In 1968 this was more of an advantage than a handicap. They were not inhibited by the prejudices of old Hollywood. They had the freedom and the confidence of pioneers. They also had Jack Nicholson.

What everyone remembers about *Easy Rider* is Jack Nicholson's speech in one of the camp-fire scenes. Yet Nicholson was not first choice for a part that Southern had originally written with Rip Torn in mind. When Torn's other commitments made that impossible, Nicholson stepped into a role he seemed to have been born to play.

He, too, had been around the Hollywood scene for a while without breaking through to fame. Born in New Jersey in 1937, he had started in the business as an MGM office boy and made his film début in *Cry Baby Killer* (1958). Nicholson applied himself to learn the craft of acting and found a living, more often than not in cheap, ephemeral pictures. It was in conjunction with Roger Corman that he developed as both an actor and a writer.

Corman made cult exploitation films (his motto: 'You must have some nudity every fifteen minutes'), including some adapted from Edgar Allan Poe's macabre gothic tales. Nicholson played in *The Terror* and *The Raven* (both 1963) among other Corman low-budget productions, and later he wrote scripts including those for *The Trip* (1967) and the Monkees' movie *Head* (1968). Intelligent, active and gregarious, he was very much 'on the scene' of the younger, alternative Hollywood set. One of the most distinctive of screen actors (which you could never say of Peter Fonda), he has claimed, jokingly or not, that he smoked giant amounts of dope to slow his speech to the trademark extended rasping drawl. His character nonetheless provides an eloquent counterpoint to the barely coherent ramblings of two dropouts.

These four can be regarded as the creative hub of the movie, and the three actors became its public face. But cinema is more than a script and visuals. It depends on people whose names may appear in the credits, but are not remembered. Other key figures will be discussed in Style and Contexts.

director as auteur

Authorship theory (auteurisme) has enriched the study of film, but it is itself problematic. The concept of the individual author as the single source of the text, the 'creator', has been challenged even in the sphere of literature, where it can be most obviously applied. In cinema, a collaborative art, it is far trickier, yet it has to be dealt with because it persists among critics and audiences alike.

Historically, like much else in Film Studies, it was a French import. The authorship perspective had been advanced as early as 1954 by François Truffaut – a director, naturally – in the influential French journal *Cahiers du Cinéma*. It was subsequently popularised by Andrew Sarris in the US, and by *Movie* magazine in Britain. *Movie's* first issue, in 1962, contained a league table of directors ranged under six headings: Great, Brilliant, Very Talented, Talented, Competent or Ambitious, and The Rest. Only two directors were in the top flight: Howard Hawks and Alfred Hitchcock, both Hollywood veterans and sturdy professionals whose careers had begun in the silent days.

Authorship theory is less a theory than an active principle for interpreting and evaluating movies. In effect, it became a means of validating Hollywood cinema, hitherto a 'low' cultural form, by applying to it criteria derived from high culture. But above all it emphasised the visual character of film by granting auteur status to the director, not the writer. A director with a personal style and/or world-view could be seen as 'transcending' the production-line material handed to him by the studio, spinning gold out of dross. Popular Hollywood movies – some of them, at least – were privileged to become art, worthy of studious attention, by virtue of the director's personal signature.

There were flaws in authorship theory, besides its consecration of the individual, that were soon exposed. Other, more objective and rigorous critical approaches soon ate into naïve auteurisme, but the concept of film authorship has become deeply embedded in film criticism and audience taste. Many cinema-goers now often identify films by directors rather than, as they once did, exclusively by stars. Commanding figures like Scorsese, Coppola and Spielberg have become recognisable brand names, superstars even, while others who straddle the line between independent and mainstream cinema (David Lynch, the Coen Brothers, Tarantino) have broken through. The vogue of authorship was an encouragement to the growth of New Hollywood.

The primary difficulty in applying authorship to *Easy Rider* is that it is the director's first film, the category in which it triumphed at Cannes. Normally, auteurisme depends on there being a substantial body of work to analyse. Furthermore, Hopper's career after *Easy Rider* was principally as an actor, increasingly in roles that played up the psychotic side of his screen personality (*Apocalypse Now, Blue Velvet, Paris Trout, Red Rock West, True Romance,* etc.). There were often echoes of *Easy Rider* in these performances, as if Billy had survived the gun blast, though brain-damaged. Indeed in the comedy/adventure movie *Flashback* (1990), in which he played an underground radical resurfacing after thirty years, there were explicit references to it. But between *Easy Rider* and *Colors* (1988) he directed only two films, the first of which was *The Last Movie* (1971).

This was a historic disaster. It was to be a story of a stunt man working in mediocre Westerns left behind in Peru after the film unit employing him has departed. Denied finance for this film by the backers of *Easy Rider,* once he had opted to play the lead as well as direct, Hopper turned to Universal. This was an old and tired company by that time largely occupied with TV production, but wishing to capitalise on the vogue for youth movies it agreed to co-finance the deal with Hopper, giving him 50% of the gross and total control.

director as auteur background

a delirious cocktail of inputs

What emerged from the anarchic filming in Peru and the long editing process in Taos, New Mexico, has been described (in Geoff Andrew's *Stranger than Paradise*) as 'a bizarre and ambitiously allegorical film ... so chaotic, self-indulgent and obscure that its critical and commercial failure ensured Hopper would not direct again till 1980! In fact it won the Golden Lion award at the Venice Film Festival and was reissued a decade later to enjoy some success. It was not actually Hopper's last movie as a director but it was a heavy black mark on his record.

It would therefore be perverse and unproductive to treat *Easy Rider* as a Dennis Hopper film in the way one might talk of a Hitchcock or Scorsese film (much as Hopper would like it). That does not negate his contribution. To write off *Easy Rider's* style as 'a simplistic amalgam of travelogue and the zoom lens', as *The Time Out Movie Guide* does, is unfair. Though Hopper's only previous involvement with direction had been limited to *The Trip*, he had immersed himself in cinema processes as more than a minor actor. What he lacked in discipline and hands-on experience he largely made up for by a willing instinct and by absorbing the lessons of contemporary non-Hollywood cinema. Lee Hill puts it this way:

> *Easy Rider's* impact was made possible by a bold synthesis of the disparate styles, moods and practice with which 60s pop culture was awash... The self-conscious use of the camera, especially the jump-cuts and zooms, also displayed the influence of the work of the various European new waves then flooding American art houses and film societies – the British Free Cinema, the French *nouvelle vague*, the Italian neo-realists from Antonioni to Fellini and the Czech New Wave. The editing built on the frenetic cutting of Richard Lester and mid-60s television advertising, and the cinéma vérité of D.A. Pennebaker and Richard Leacock. The underground films of Jonas Mekas, Stan Brakhage, Andy Warhol and others suggested seemingly infinite possibilities of cinematic expression, some of which *Easy Rider* exploited and developed.

This is a delirious cocktail of inputs, which makes Hopper an eclectic rather than an original director. If Hopper seized on this miscellany of current anti-realist mise-en-scène

influences opportunistically, it is also true that the film's content hardly called for the smooth, eye-level look of the classic Hollywood feature. Such narrative climaxes as the bad acid trip in New Orleans could only be served by an anti-realist mise-en-scène (see Style: Mise-en-scène). Impressions of the landscape, too, are shot dramatically and matched with soundtrack music, precisely to escape the feel of a plodding travelogue. And it's worth adding that Hopper, however wildly he behaved, however much he exaggerated his own contribution, put his heart and soul into the movie.

By any strict standard, this does not make him an auteur. But he is no amateur either. He makes his presence felt in *Easy Rider*: as director, as actor, as to some extent a writer and as a selector of the songs – as forming the mould for what he has since become, that is, a kind of 'gonzo' wicked uncle figure, a cultish player of startling oddballs, still crazy (though less libertarian) after all these years.

narrative & form

film narrative

In *Film Art: An Introduction*, David Bordwell and Kristin Thompson take narrative to mean *'a chain of events in a cause-effect relationship occurring in time and space.'* More simply, a story. Hollywood cinema has always been a narrative cinema, though cinema is not inherently compelled to tell stories. There is such a thing as anti-narrative film. Such experiments can be formally intriguing, but they are seldom entertaining and attract small audiences. Hollywood is a cinema of mass entertainment, dedicated to shaping stories that build large global audiences and make its economy possible.

The narrative structure of a film resides in the way it articulates its story, choosing the elements and arranging them so that they fashion a chain of meaning. For the critical analysis of film, it is a crucial abstraction. Sometimes it is referred to as the 'deep structure', the inner framework beneath what is visible on the screen.

In Hollywood cinema, narrative structures more often than not adopt the explication/ complication/ resolution pattern. That is, an initial situation, or 'equilibrium', is disrupted by complications that give rise to drama, suspense or comedy. These are played out until finally a new equilibrium is restored by a dénouement to produce what film theorists call narrative closure and others 'a happy ending', or at least a definite one.

A typical structure might be: 'boy meets girl; boy loses girl; boy gets girl.' Romantic comedy serves up this recipe over and over again. Other genres repeat their tried and trusted storylines, though there are 'open' or ambiguous endings as well, avoiding closure and designed to leave the audience in doubt. These are less common in the Hollywood product than in art house movies such as the Japanese *Rashomon*, poorly remade by Hollywood as *The Outrage* (1964), where no final truth emerges.

you can follow Billy and Wyatt on the map

Two primary decisions determine the narrative structure in film: the selection of shots that will appear on the screen and their sequencing (the narrative 'flow'). In the editing process (see Style: Editing), the footage chosen to compose the release print is assembled to form a coherent narrative. In principle several different movies could be made from the same footage, and in fact release prints do sometimes circulate in differing versions.

What is more, seemingly dissimilar films may share a basic narrative structure. Much Hollywood narrative works to track the progress of a sympathetic hero and heroine through adversity to a permanent pair-bonding, or to restore a divided family, even in ostensibly quite different types of film – in *The Sound of Music* as well as *Jaws*, *High Noon* and *The Long Kiss Goodnight*. The final equilibrium invites the audience to share the characters' final happiness vicariously; not to imagine, beyond the closure imposed by the ending, breakfast table quarrels, death or divorce.

As a rule, too, Hollywood narratives are linear, unfolding in chronological time. There are exceptions (*Reservoir Dogs*, for instance), and flashbacks that briefly interrupt 'natural' time are familiar enough to be easily read by audiences. Also science fiction movies challenge our usual understanding of time and space. But overall Hollywood favours narrative patterns that correspond to the viewer's own real-world sense of logic, order and progression, satisfyingly united in closure.

narrative in easy rider

Easy Rider is a hybrid: not exactly a 'closed' narrative, however final death may be. Too much is left unresolved. It helped establish the genre of road movies (see Contexts: Road Movies), in which the journey is more important than the destination. But its narrative is not complex or difficult, mainly because a journey is itself already a traditional kind of narrative structure. Mostly the narrative is linear and chronological, though less fluent than the Hollywood norm. You can follow Billy and Wyatt on a map. The heroes' vague dream of reaching Florida signifies only that the land ends there. The story equates to whatever happens on the road. Dense plotting would be redundant. The narrative rhythms follow Wyatt's movement... more important than direction

repudiation of objective time and scenes are paced according to the prevailing emotional temperature ('vibes') rather than standard plot logic.

Moreover, the story takes the heroes through a succession of experiences that teach them little except the hopelessness of the quest in the first place. The preferred templates for analysing narrative structure – like those designed by Propp and Lévi–Strauss, move archetypal characters through stock situations ('narrative functions' in Proppian language) which progressively resolve what is at stake. In the end something is learned, or won. Order has been restored. Conflicts and contradictions are sewn up. By contrast, *Easy Rider* presents only division, blind ignorance and futile deaths.

NARRATIVE AS JOURNEY

In the US especially, narrative as journey has long been a favourite device for intertwining myth with history. Narrative structures needed to be understood historically, not just formally. A nation founded on pioneering momentum and exploration as well as conquest, America harnessed the theme of travel and discovery early on. Two classic American novels of the nineteenth century, *Moby Dick* (1851) and *The Adventures of Huckleberry Finn* (1884) are mapped out as journeys. Huck Finn has a comparable urge to Billy and Wyatt – 'They ain't gonna sivilise me' – at the finish of his journey, and opts to keep moving, beyond the inhibiting reach of social control.

The mythic journey, wherever it takes place, is always an obsessive, difficult search for America and a simultaneous search for one's self. The nineteenth-century poet Walt Whitman, 'facing west from California's shore' projecting himself around the world and all its marvels in his imagination, hankered for what was 'still unfound', his own American identity.

Movement in America happened for solid historical reasons: to settle, populate, work and govern a continent. But it fast accumulated a positive worth of its own. From Whitman to the Beats of a century later, movement has often been more vital than direction to American artists. In the 1953 biker movie, *The Wild One*, Marlon Brando as the young rebel declares 'You don't go anywhere. You just go!' The nomadic American hero doesn't need to know where he's going. Going, or leaving, is the objective.

So *Easy Rider* draws on long-established strengths: not only audience memories of the Western but the entrenched formula of travel and spontaneous adventure. Yet Billy and Wyatt are reversing the historical momentum, travelling from west to east. This hints at something perverse and wrong about their trip, just as the drug deal does (not the drugs but the deal, a get-rich-quick stunt which feels too mercenary for a pair of freedom-seekers). So the narrative begins by querying the value of the quest. It resembles more an escape, across a territory where everyone they meet is a stranger, either marginal, confused or lethally hostile.

The route on the map is erratic, but *Easy Rider* is not an undisciplined, free-form work. It develops structurally through combining the time-honoured journey pattern with a variety of film techniques, some of them unorthodox (see Style). As illustration, it is worth examining first of all one of the salient structuring motifs of *Easy Rider*, the camp-fire scenes.

THE CAMP-FIRE SCENES

For their first overnight, Bill and Wyatt have to camp out because a 76 motel keeper, frightened by their appearance, has rejected them, switching his neon sign from 'Vacancy' to 'No Vacancy'. As they ride off, Billy yelling 'You asshole!', flash cuts chop up time and space and the flickering camp fire is introduced. Camping out is plausibly motivated by the same opposition that pulses at the centre of the film. But the camp-fire setting already has a symbolic force.

In pioneer days a camp fire meant light, warmth and a means of cooking food in the shadowy surroundings of what was often feared as a savage wilderness. Camp-fire scenes are popular in Westerns, where they often supply a comfort zone for male bonding. Around the camp fire, stories can be told and feelings expressed which elsewhere, in daylight, would be held back. But antagonisms, too, often reveal themselves. In the darkness and the open air, pretences are dropped. The camp fire is a cherished tableau in the iconography of the American West.

It is therefore a mythical environment, not just a physical one. And it is an appropriate one for two outlaw characters who have deserted the city (albeit on high-powered machines). The countryside is hidden by night, stressing their isolation together, face to face in the firelight. The differences between them, and their unspoken wish not to let those differences matter, emerge in fragments of druggy conversation.

The first night sketches out the relationship. Billy anticipates the future delights that their big score will buy them: 'a Mardi Gras queen', 'a groovy dinner'. He mocks the sacred spirit of the camp-fire myth itself: 'out here in the wilderness, fighting Indians and cowboys on every side'. It is one more clue that he's a wired raver with no special concerns outside himself. Wyatt by contrast is quiet and reflective – 'pulling inside', as Billy puts it. Wyatt's reply is 'I'm just getting my thing together'. This over-used phrase of the time cloudily indicating an underlying hope or plan, a search for identity or meaning, contrasts with Billy's coarse, fleshly ambitions (Manny Farber calls Billy the 'Sancho Panza' of the film, after Don Quixote's appetite-driven companion).

As further flash cuts forward the scene to morning, the sun strikes through bare roof beams. Wyatt is viewed in a series of shots observing bits of debris (the carcass of an old car, a compass or watch, a worn, tattered book) as if trying to puzzle out what they mean. Perhaps what they evoke is the migration of early Americans across the land, moving on or dying out. Billy's and Wyatt's odyssey is not new. And it is not guaranteed success.

The second camp-fire scene occurs the following night, by which time they have picked up a hitch hiker, designated The Stranger. He rides on Wyatt's pillion, not Billy's, as George Hanson will do later. Billy, as usual, is suspicious, especially when the Stranger fills the gas tank where the cash is stored. But the Stranger is (as Billy might put it) grooving on his own vibes; he has a secretive, mystical air. The camp-fire setting, a ruined stone shack, is introduced via another set of flash cuts, after a long, slow pan at dusk over dramatically silhouetted rock formations in Monument Valley, an iconic setting recognisable from John Ford Westerns (see Style: Cinematography). The three are alone together in a darkening desert landscape. A joint is passed around, and prompts them to talk.

The dialogue again stresses difference rather than unity. In answer to Billy's insistent questioning, the Stranger explains that he is a refugee from the city. 'It doesn't make any difference what city. All cities are alike. That's why I'm out here now.'

Billy is showing his inner anxieties again, and has to be reminded that 'the people this place belongs to are buried right under you ... You could be a trifle polite.' Wyatt then asks the Stranger if he ever wanted to be anyone else. Stranger: 'I'd like to try Porky Pig.' Wyatt tells him, 'I never wanted to be anybody else.'

This is strange, because Wyatt is unassertive, a man without strong opinions or much personality who can take or leave whatever comes along, while Billy remains a grumpy and paranoid critic. The Stranger, like them, is a refugee from the city. Unlike them, he has a goal. Disconnection makes them separate, and the camera cuts between them, framing them individually in close-up or reargrounding Billy, to underline their apartness. With little common ground to share, there is not much to say; more flash cuts show the morning sunshine refracted through the trees. They're on the road again.

By the fourth night, after their arrest and brief imprisonment in Las Vegas, New Mexico, George Hanson is riding along, and the camp-fire interlude is built around Hanson's introduction to the countercultural delights of marijuana. Hanson is a Southern liberal black sheep with a drink problem. We know he is a good guy because he has done work for the American Civil Liberties Union – the ACLU. He may not be hip in the way Billy and Wyatt are – words like 'dude' and 'groovy' tickle him – yet he is easily persuaded to smoke a joint while listening to some of Billy's vacant chatter.

```
Billy
        No, man. Like, hey, man. Wow! I was watching
        this object, man-like-like- the satellite that
        we saw the other night, right? And like it was
        just going right across the sky, man. And then,
        I mean, it just suddenly - uh - (laughs) it
        just changed direction and went-uh-whizzing
        right off, man.
```

narrative

the authentic narcotised expression of a pothead

George and Wyatt
in a restful two-shot,
Billy out of frame.
Jack Nicholson wears
a college sweater and the
authentic narcotised
expression of a pothead

Billy explains that this object flashed three times at him before it vanished. It is as near as he gets to a visionary statement; as Wyatt points out, he is stoned out of his mind. But it is still only a piece of communications technology he sees. Hanson, in the spirit of the novice smoker, performs a riff on Billy's tale. It sounds as if it has been cobbled together from urban folklore, hokey SF plots and sensationalised media reports (it seems the secretary who typed up the script in New York was a UFO fan). It is plainly satirical: not what Hanson believes, but a psychotropic fantasy, a what-if yarn.

George
> Well, they are people just like us - from
> within our own solar system. Except that their
> society is more highly evolved. I mean, they
> don't have no wars, they got no monetary
> system, they don't have any leaders, because,
> I mean, each man is a leader. I mean each man
> - because of their technology, they are able
> to feed, clothe, house and transport
> themselves equally - and with no effort.

Looked at closely, though, this sounds less like George's mild mockery of Billy than a glancing liberal joke aimed at the Sixties' utopian dream of peace and love. The mournful suggestion that 'the Dream is over' was widely echoed at this time. Altamont (a Rolling Stones' concert which went awry when Hell's Angels killed a black fan) and the Manson murders (when Manson's 'family' killed six people including Sharon Tate, Roman Polanski's pregnant wife) were among the events of 1969, and none of the three main characters in *Easy Rider* possesses any faith in an alternative future. Their movement is always away from, not towards, any kind of organised society. As the scene ends 'Don't Bogart Me' pours in on the soundtrack, keeping the tone light.

The fourth camp-fire scene features George Hanson's famous speech, easily the most didactic in the film. It occurs after the tense and menacing visit to a restaurant where local white trash have insulted them. George begins by saying, 'This used to be a helluva good country. I can't understand what's gone wrong with it.'

The local relevance of these words is clear. They refer to the hate waves at the restaurant. But George is speaking generally, and though the sentiment is appealing it is worth asking what he means. A man of his age would be able to call on personal experience and memories stretching back no earlier than the last years of the Great Depression, the late 1930s. These were followed, over thirty years, by the cataclysm of the Second World War and the daily anxieties of the Cold War, then by Vietnam. Personally, he has lived his entire life in a troubled, not a golden, age. Where then is the past golden age?

It must be the imaginary golden age of freedom and self-fulfilment which historically never was, but which, as one of the visionary impulses that inspired the settlement of America and the founding of the nation, continues as a mythic ideal. No actual America can equal this paragon, so the present sentimentalises the past. Present ills are regarded as a sad, puzzling Fall from a perfect state. Although American history is crowded with oppression and injustice, despite what the Declaration of Independence promises – a right to 'Life, Liberty, and the pursuit of Happiness' – the past is a convenient alibi.

This strain of conservative nostalgia in George's discourse is an inkling of failure. With no concept of an alternative future, alienated from a society which they can never completely evade, all the heroes can do is use themselves up on an aimless trip. The camp-fire scenes chart a progressive disillusion, as Billy and Wyatt run out of both geographical and narrative space.

George next launches into as something approaching a social analysis, after Billy wonders why the rednecks are 'scared'.

```
George
      Oh, they're not scared of you. They're scared
      of what you represent.
Billy
      Hey, man. All we represent to them, man, is
      somebody who needs a haircut.
```

```
George
      Oh, no... What you represent to them is freedom.
Billy
      What the hell's wrong with freedom, man.
      That's what it's all about.
George
      Oh, yeah; that's right - that's what it's
      about all right... But talking about it and
      being it - that's two different things... I
      mean, it's real hard to be free when you're
      bought and sold in the marketplace. 'Course,
      don't ever tell anybody... that they're not
      free, cause they're gonna get real busy
      killin' and maimin' to prove that they are.
```

This is a fair insight, marking George as the articulate, educated lawyer, whose grim prognosis will be borne out. But again it is not a new idea. As early as 1835 a French observer of the young republic, Alexis de Tocqueville, had cautioned against 'the tyranny of the majority': 'under the absolute sway of an individual despot the body was attacked in order to subdue the soul... but such is not the course adopted by tyranny in democratic republics; there the body is left free, and the soul enslaved'. H.D. Thoreau, the nineteenth-century Transcendentalist writer, and role-model for hippies, denounced (in *Slavery in Massachusetts*, 1854) not only the Fugitive Slave Law that forced free states to return escaped slaves but the mental enslavement to bigotry of those who imagined themselves free. Minorities and outgroups in America have faced persecution more frequently than respect or even tolerance.

Likewise, the violence of the Southerners in *Easy Rider* displays the fear of 'otherness' (that perceived difference that allows outgroups to be stigmatised and stereotyped) and the frenzied reaction it provokes. Thoreau also wrote in his seminal work *Walden* (1854) that 'the mass of men lead lives of quiet desperation'; by the late 1960s the 'silent majority' seemed desperate to crack down on dissent, while some radicals of the extreme New Left - militant, and militantly opposed by the establishment

– had been 'bringing the war back home' in heavy confrontations. The polarity easily led to violence, and stray dropouts were not immune. The American South, with its heritage of lynch law, is partly a special case, readier to resort to rough justice. But the antagonisms were nationwide. George's golden vision of what America 'used to be' is an orphaned wish.

It does, though, help confirm the growing sense that the journey is a voyage to nowhere. Discouraging truths are revealed in the moments of isolation and confession with which the camp-fire scenes shape the narrative.

By **the final camp-fire scene** the dream *is* over for Wyatt. George is dead. The acid trip in New Orleans was a nightmare. The longer the journey lasts, the bleaker and uglier the mood becomes. Wyatt sums it up in three words.

```
Wyatt
      -we blew it.
Billy
      What? Huh? Wha-wha-wha- That's what it's all
      about, man. I mean, like, you know, you go for
      the big money, man - and then you're free. You
      dig? (Laughs.)
CUT TO: mcs - Billy (lying down) - he sits up RIGHT.
Wyatt
      We blew it.
```

Wyatt doesn't blame their attackers. 'Blowing it' means getting it wrong, missing your chance. Billy is appetite-driven. He hasn't understood. What he says could be the motto of any young hopeful from the city. It is not a countercultural statement. Billy hasn't changed, and that's his problem. Wyatt has, and that's his.

The camp-fire scenes thread the pattern of a 'lost quest' into the narrative. Even Wyatt can't explain the loss. Though introspective, he has the limited vocabulary of someone impelled by forces beyond his reasoning. But he does know, as the audience must know by now, that the search was vain. The camp fire has not drawn people together and warmed their hearts; it has marked the stages of disintegration.

narrative

'a little distance'

The vertical flames
of the camp-fire
divide the screen space,
putting 'a little
distance' between
Billy and Wyatt

specific form

Structures can be found for any kind of narrative, for published fiction and as equally for cinema and the theatre. They are the articulations interior to the text that shape and direct the narrative. But there is a vital difference between a novel and a movie. Both media employ language, but only cinema uses moving images, which are its specific form. They are more central to the narration than the dialogue is. Semiotic skills are required for a close reading of film. And since the cinematic image has no single language, no master code, it has to be read largely in terms of its connotations

These in turn will be governed by a variety of filmic codes (lighting, camera angle, mise-en-scène, etc.) and extra-cinematic factors (assumptions about gender roles, for example) as well as by individual response (see Contexts). Every visual detail has meaning. We get some idea of Wyatt's confused identity when we see what he is wearing: biker leathers over braided or floral hippy-style shirts, plus the flag, emblem of patriotism, on his clothes and bike. Billy's fringed buckskin and Wild West hat associate him with the frontier scout or hunter. More significantly, much of Kovács's cinematography dwells on the physical environment (see Style: Cinematography).

It has been said of the Western movie that its true subject is the American landscape – the mountains, prairies, forests, deserts and valleys that frame the action. Those extended sequences that track riders across the terrain have enormous lyrical power. Yet they're not narrative waste. They show the spacious, overwhelming beauty of the land; they also materialise the hidden dangers and obstacles, definite story functions, encountered on the path to narrative resolution.

And the Western provides many of the cinematic codes at work in *Easy Rider*. It begins in the West, at the dead end of frontier settlement. As they travel – they never get far beyond the Mississippi – the camera pays tribute to the American West. It is a natural landscape, not a studio one. But it is still a movie landscape, recognisable to movie audiences who have never seen it firsthand but who know their Westerns, replete with connotations.

specific form

There's one large ironic difference, besides the inverted, West-to-East route. The purpose of the traditional Western screen hero (though it makes him redundant) is to build law, order and civilisation from a wilderness. Billy's and Wyatt's aim is to put civilisation behind them. The settings are integral to the tale. Shot with the bikes in motion, often against the sun, they show grand, variegated scenery and miles of empty distance. In a mechanised age, the roads across California, Arizona and New Mexico are near-deserted and communities few and far between. At sunset the great sandstone blocks of Monument Valley, home of the Navajo, turn the screen into a shadow play, with the travellers as flimsy cut-out marionettes. At most times the land, though awesome, offers no comfort to them. It has buried so many of their predecessors.

There is the sense of a relationship with the land yet to be achieved, after countless generations (the hippies are making a probably doomed effort). Its prominence in the mise-en-scène suggests a dramatic play-off between the vastness of the space and the limitations of its human inhabitants. This is part of the myth, too. In America the land has been fought over, apportioned by government, bought and sold, abused or neglected. It still retains its lasting spiritual attraction for those who dream of the past. And it is probably the best natural subject for big-screen colour photography.

Easy Rider echoes the Western, but the classic Western hero, though a loner, is self-redeeming. His life (or in some cases his death) is justified by the good he brings about. It is a definable goal – the defeat of the bad guys, the establishment of justice, community harmony. Billy and Wyatt lack a goal. Their rebellion, if it is one, is precisely against the goal-oriented treadmill of regular urban life.

They ride through country that offers them no home and no answers, that outlasts them. This expressive use of landscape iconography has to be read in the context of its traditional meanings in American culture, and especially in film. But though moving images are the specific form of film, in *Easy Rider* they are heavily underpinned by the accompanying soundtrack music. For a discussion of this, see Style: Music.

character

'Character' in fiction is a problematic notion. Characters are not real people, though they may, especially in a graphic medium like cinema, cause us to suspend disbelief. Sitting in the dark, it is hard not to respond to them, and judge them, as if they were real. 'Psychological realism' may give the illusion of real-life depth and complexity, encouraging the audience to take up involved moral attitudes towards flickering shadows on screen. Character in this sense also goes with the star system and the loyalties of fandom.

Genre films need to use stock figures: it would be strange to think of, say, Darth Vader as a character in the full sense. But critics and audiences often demand more than archetypes and caricatures. And though all fictional characters, however 'lifelike', are figments of the imagination, it is reasonable to criticise the *quality of representation* of characters who are drawn from a dull pool of ready-made stereotypes.

Alternatively, structural analyses may treat characters as 'narrative functions', i.e. in terms of how they advance the story rather than as mimetic portraits. This can be useful. It offsets the temptation to treat characters as living people – 'naïve realism'. But it is a dry and limited approach. It does not account for audience emotions, such as empathy and identification, which are linked to the perception of character. And, as a formal method, it has little to say about the play of ideology in a text. But character does have a semiotic function. It signifies.

Billy and Wyatt deal cocaine and travel together, but they are differentiated throughout. First of all, they are distinguished from each other by appearance. Billy, squat and edgy, looks like the wild man; Wyatt is quieter and relatively well groomed, with conspicuously shorter hair. He wears modern biking leathers.

The differences are continued in how they speak and behave. Billy is rude and querulous at times, at others boisterously playful. Wyatt is quieter, more introverted and generally so laconic, vague and 'gone' that he scarcely exists. His idea of an 'idea' in a bordello is 'Let's go outside'. His passivity makes him easygoing but drains him of a definite identity. He may be more thoughtful, though he says little of interest till he decides that 'We blew it! If they are somehow buddies, they display none of the intimate fellowship that we find in the close male couples of *Midnight Cowboy* or the excellent TV series *Starsky and Hutch*. From the viewpoint of psychological realism they are little developed, mainly because they have no history, no family, no tangible network of relationships with the wider world.

Still, they have a naturalistic existence on the screen. They are not fairy-tale symbolic figures, the way Darth Vader is. Nor are they pure archetypes, like many heroes of the Western. But what they signify, personally and in their interaction with others, goes beyond their individuality.

Historically, they fit the category of the classic American seeker-hero, the 'isolato' as Herman Melville called him, who deserts society to seek 'the ungraspable phantom of life': the template for the American existential hero, whose uncompromising, romantic quest for freedom, meaning and identity always brings trouble and adventure. (One of the early mooted titles for *Easy Rider* was *The Loners*.) The isolato defines himself against the majority who accept life as it has been handed to them. His journey can, and often does, end in catastrophe.

They are also two unattached young white males, committed to non-attachment. Inarticulate drifters who almost deny themselves the social tool of language, they have left behind more than the city and its host of willing slaves. They have rejected the developmentalist notion of a masculine progress towards maturity via the acceptance a staged series of responsibilities – work, marriage, fatherhood and so on. Because they have not considered serious alternatives, they open themselves to the charge of a prolonged adolescence – not a privilege for all. Their characters, in short, mirror the cultural assumptions of their age, gender and ethnicity. They are doing what a man wants to do and can do, rather than what he's gotta do, but age is a key factor (see Contexts: Class, Race & Gender). The duck-hunters (apparently) who kill them are equally white and male, but older.

Lastly, they represent some of the typical lifestyle options of the counterculture of the late 1960s. Their groovy idioms, casual use of leisure drugs, dress and behaviour belong to the generation that asked some urgent questions – even if some of the answers were off-track.

contrary tendencies dividing the States

The counterculture did throw up leaders, stars and false prophets, but it had a broad democratic base among the young. Growing up to be a clone of your parents, listening to Bing Crosby or going to church in your Sunday best were suddenly not an inevitable fate. It was much easier to rebel if you were affluent, of course, and big commercial interests were soon riding on the back of the counterculture. It was never immune to the establishment it scorned. It bred its own set of much derided clichés. All the same, it rediscovered the politics of pleasure, the celebratory spirit of the Woodstock Nation. Billy and Wyatt are a pair of not-too-bright dropouts, but they are harmless dropouts, 'doing their own thing'.

George Hanson is the most fleshed-out character, the most 'written'. He is not in the picture for long, but we learn a lot about him. This is appropriate. He is educated, he is fluent, and, as a character, he embodies the contrary tendencies that were dividing the States. His greater complexity sums up the liberal dilemma at moments of crisis: to devise an ordered society that will not be a repressive society. He works for the ACLU, but pays off the cops; comes from a respected local family, but regularly lands in the drunk tank. He has never realised his Mardi Gras dream. Despite his sophistication, he gets boyishly excited at the thought of visiting prostitutes ('US prime'). Straddling two value-systems helps his understanding while it weakens his chances of survival. He does not live long once he is off his home territory. Liberalism is vulnerable in the South.

All three principal characters are defined against the racist rednecks who label them freaks and enemies. They are the extreme and pathological Southern fringe of Middle America who represent its violent subconscious urges to trash nonconformity and assert its own righteousness. Character in *Easy Rider* is drawn in a range of tones, but always has strong social implications.

style

style as signature

'The use a film makes of the medium', write Bordwell and Thompson, 'cannot be studied apart from the film's use of narrative... form', since 'style interacts with the formal system'. In other words, style is not an envelope wrapped around the film's content, but integral with meaning.

In literature, style is generally apparent to the reader. Though the death of the author has been announced and the role of context creatively expanded, authors live on in their individual use of language, or 'idiolect'. It is easy to recognise the prose style of, say, Dickens, Hemingway or Martin Amis. Vocabulary, sentence and paragraph structure, imagery and other linguistic elements constitute a personal 'signature'.

Film is different. It is a collaborative and multi-media art. No one 'signature' is necessarily dominant. Auteurisme favours the pre-eminence of the director, and there certainly are some directors who stamp their style on the movie like an autograph. But more usual in Hollywood's history is a studio or house style, with the director as skilled contract professional rather than creator. It can be a sophisticated style, but it is one that does not call attention to itself, since to do so would be to snap the illusion that keeps the audience involved.

Primarily, film style means visual style, the 'treatment' that decides the tone and meaning of a picture. In principle a screenplay can be filmed in a number of ways, each one inflecting its meaning differently according to the chosen style. A scene shot from a distance in the rain will have a different significance from the same scene, with the same dialogue, close-up and sunny. Style is decisive, and the most fundamental concept for analysing visual style is mise-en-scène.

mise-en-scène

By mise-en-scène is meant whatever appears in the frame, the complete ensemble of visual elements – from shot composition, lighting, set dressing, expressive use of locations, movement and gesture, right down to costume and make-up. The term (literally 'put in the scene') is derived from theatre. However, there is a root difference. Where a play is performed live, a film is assembled from prerecorded footage cut and spliced in the editing process. Editing – or montage – has to be considered along with mise-en-scène in any discussion of visual style (see Editing, below).

The characteristics of the mise-en-scène may be equated with a genre, or subgenre, as well as with a studio style or a director. The typical mise-en-scène of *film noir*, for instance, relies on low-key lighting, drenching the screen in shadow, often making an urban environment made appear bleak and menacing. In studio set-ups what appears in the mise-en-scène is artificial: a sound stage can be dressed to represent a city street, a farmyard or the moon. In Westerns the mise-en-scène takes advantage of the natural splendours of America to complement a mythological retelling of history, with extensive location shooting. But even when what the camera records are real-world surroundings, mise-en-scène is always a cinematic device, carrying narrative and thematic meaning and a certain attitude.

visual style

Easy Rider is heavily location-shot. Hopper records that only one set was built, to represent the hippy commune. As a rule, location shooting is one of the marks of realism in cinema, lending a solid physical context to a fictional story. Equally and conversely, it can heighten the expressive or symbolic potential of a setting, like the city as 'asphalt jungle' in crime movies. In the predominantly visual opening scenes of *Easy Rider* (there are sound effects and music but no English dialogue till after the credits), the cardinal image of the city is not LA itself but its airport. The framing of this sequence calls attention to the aircraft which swoop deafeningly in with their passenger loads, intensive and purposeful, while Billy and Wyatt trade with the Connection. The Connection ducks as the huge, powerful machines pass overhead, as if the mechanical force they exert is pressing him down in his seat. Their noise blocks communication and their shapes disfigure the sky (as the B52 bombers were invading the sky in Vietnam and, in 1969, neutral Cambodia).

This early image of urban stress, however, does not stand alone. It has to be read against subsequent, contrasting ones. The open road and the great outdoors supply most of the settings and, as in the Western, they are much more than settings. The familiar American scattering of towns, gas stations, motels and farms appears mainly as a passing tableau seen from moving motorbikes, slipping away as the next stretch of free country is reached. With no planes in the overarching sky and little traffic on the road, Billy and Wyatt can taste a kind of detached freedom, and the mise-en-scène follows their passage between stops in rhythmical sequences that stress space and motion.

The panoramas of the American south-west, Monument Valley among them, are filmed to fill the screen with their traditional grandeur and isolation; alternatively, a travelling camera keeps pace with the riders, picturing their enjoyment of the ride and their occasional antics. Wyatt and Billy may not belong to the land (Wyatt respects the farmer who does), may not even appreciate it much, but it gives them a breathing space. The playfulness will vanish later, as they encounter the land's hostile inhabitants. At night the camera moves in closer still to catch the talk by the camp fire. Cuts, not **fades** or **dissolves**, link the shots, and the cutting pace intensifies towards the end of the film, as calamity approaches.

Easy Rider employs a blend of styles, which vary according to narrative requirements. Three basic stylistic modes can be identified: **semidocumentary**, lyrical realism and fast montage.

SEMIDOCUMENTARY

This technique has antecedents at least as far back as the Italian neo-realism that flourished after the Second World War. Neo-realism exploited location shooting in ordinary surroundings, grainy photography and the presence of non-professional actors. Such films as *Bicycle Thieves* (1948), though fictional, mimicked the raw, unrehearsed quality of the non-fiction film. By 1969 cinéma-vérité, sometimes called fly-on-the-wall documentary, had access to newer and lighter recording technology – such as the hand-held camera – which gave it an intimate, eavesdropping feel. D.A. Pennebaker's documentary coverage of Bob Dylan's British tour, *Don't Look Back* (1967) successfully employed vérité to chronicle the hectic road life of a countercultural star. For much of the time, *Easy Rider* borrows this idiom to project a low-key naturalism.

LYRICAL REALISM

A mise-en-scène that exploits landscape draws on the iconography of the West to designate an emotional and spiritual bond between the American hero and the wild territory of the frontier. At this level, *Easy Rider* partakes of what *Newsweek* magazine called 'the romance of rootlessness'. Apart from its central place in the visual lexicon of the Western movie, and the quoting of John Ford's monumentalism in *Easy Rider*, America's geophysical glory has long been a treasured subject for writers, painters, composers and photographers. Always in the popular imagination the country, whether desert or garden, forbidding or uplifting, stands for nature conceived as a quasi-religious force identified with the national character and the epic version of its history.

The mixture of styles demonstrates an openness to both experimentation and tradition. In an interview with the *Evergreen Review* after the film's first New York showing, Dennis Hopper eagerly pronounced on his theory of film direction:

> I believe what Cocteau said: 'ninety-eight percent of all creation is accident, one per cent intellect and one per cent logic'. I believe that: you must keep free for things to happen, wait for the accident and then learn how to use the accident.

Jean Cocteau was a French writer, artist and film-maker (and drug user) whose work in cinema favoured dream states and a 'poetic' mise-en-scène. (The immediate context for the quote is the use of water-damaged film by Hopper in the acid-trip montage.) Cocteau's name may have been shamelessly hijacked to lend credibility to Hopper's work, but it does suit Hopper's aleatory (chance or random) method in the Mardi Gras, where fast montage (or 'impact edits') pays jumbled homage to European art cinema and to American underground film. There are reasons for this, apart from any aspiration to high-art status: namely, the interest of the Mardi Gras episode has in the visual representation of extreme mental states.

THE NEW ORLEANS SEQUENCE

The New Orleans sequence lasts about fifteen minutes, and includes some of the 16mm footage taken at Mardi Gras itself in February 1968, before a shooting script was finalised with Terry Southern in New York. This initial footage was finally incorporated with the results of principal photography at the editing stage.

It immediately follows George's murder, and the discovery by Billy and Wyatt of the brothel card he had earlier shown them as they check out his wallet. A jump cut then switches the scene to New Orleans, and appetising close-ups of cooking food. It is time for the 'groovy dinner' and the setting looks perfect, an epicurean restaurant. The scene is lit with a rich, steady golden glow, resembling the mise-en-scène of a seductive food commercial, as if promising satisfaction after the hard nights on the road. New Orleans is generally thought of as a cultured and vibrant Southern city, with a pleasure-driven interest in jazz, food and erotic delights; visually, the scene accords with this reputation.

But it is accompanied by music that undercuts it: the Electric Prunes' 'Kyrie Eleison' ('Lord have mercy') from their 1968 *Mass in F Minor*. The thin, plaintive music is in tune with Wyatt's mood rather than Billy's; he is more silent, abstracted and withdrawn than usual, while Billy smokes, gulps wine, grins and wolfs his food. Most shots are separate, single close-ups. Once again, the disparity points to travelling companions rather than close-bonded buddies. All the same, when Billy wants to go to Madame Tinkertoy's House of Blue Lights for 'just one drink' in honour of George Hanson because 'he would have wanted us to', Wyatt passively agrees.

One drink, of course, leads to another. New Orleans is an alluring tourist destination, and here they are essentially behaving like tourists. Whatever

Billy's pretext, bordellos are more the province of tired businessmen (or lawyers) than freewheeling hipsters. What they get, though, in an extended montage, is not a regular tourist experience.

The House of Blue Lights is first of all signified by a rapid interplay of Christian and sexual iconography – paintings, prints, murals. These ornate and decadent furnishings hint at something more disturbing than commercial sex. When some ladies of the house appear, Billy gets into the spirit of things while Wyatt prowls at a distance, arms folded, then sits down, shaking his head. Fast cutting, and no sound but the harsh chords of 'Kyrie Eleison', choreograph the scene as a bizarre spectacle, the colourful, opulent interior of the house suggesting a stage set. This is no lively orgy, more a discontinuous dumb show or masquerade with the characters momentarily sealed off from the audience. The jump cuts and brief shots render the impression of still images in a flipped-through album.

Dialogue resumes as Wyatt, looking off-screen, murmurs 'If God did not exist it would be necessary to invent him', raising a snort from Billy who is 'a little smashed'. Whether Wyatt knows it or not, the saying is Voltaire's, signifying a crisis of faith, a need to believe in a world that offers few grounds for belief. He drifts, fingering a stone carving inscribed 'The paths of glory lead but to the grave'. A flash cut, possibly a clairvoyant insight of Wyatt's, shows a burning bike as he is reading a plaque on the wall: 'Death only closes a man's reputation and determines it as good or bad'.

The dark side of carnival has invaded the house of pleasure, and these heavy-handed reminders of mortality overshadow the next sequence, in which Wyatt and Billy pair off with Mary and Karen. The camera cuts between the couples, Billy and Karen smooching while Wyatt, looking pale and remote, can barely converse with Mary. On separate pieces of film, they are virtually in separate universes. And they are scarcely a joyous foursome when, at Wyatt's prompting, they hit the street. It is at this juncture, at the pre-Lenten festival of Mardi Gras (Shrove Tuesday), that the style becomes markedly self-conscious as the narrative enters the troubled waters of sex, death and religion.

Festivals celebrating the death of winter and the rebirth of nature have a far longer history than Christianity. Like the Roman Saturnalia, they give a temporary, permissive release from normal social constraints – carnival, 'the world turned upside down'. In the Christian calendar, Shrove Tuesday is the last chance for self-indulgence before the austere self-denial of Lent. The Mardi Gras celebrations in New Orleans, world-famous for their well-organised public displays, serve the inevitable wish to depose authority and let the good times roll (some of the wackier countercultural agendas in effect sought a permanent carnival). What ensues, to borrow words of the novelist Bill Pronzini, is 'a kind of madness', an 'uncontrollable atmosphere'.

Demythologising Mardi Gras in his 1981 novel *Masques*, Pronzini wrote of fear rather than fun, focusing on the sleaze, aggression and cruel trickery that can accompany carnival. For sure, New Orleans, the high spot of the journey, proves a bad trip for Billy and Wyatt. As they join the crowds, the hand-held camera tracks them, while a (**diegetic**) band plays 'When the Saints Go Marching In'. Blown up, the 16mm frames have the unpolished, home-movie look of cinéma-vérité. At the same time, the erratic light values and colour temperatures in the jump-cut succession of shots add to the phantasmagoric spectacle of floats and costumes. The two couples wander, buy drinks, neck, observe the parade; but it is not the spirit of carnival that grips them.

FAST MONTAGE

The LSD trip. Of all the favoured leisure drugs circulating in the various subcultures of the 1960s, LSD lent itself most readily to the founding of a cult. Ken Kesey, who had first tried at as a medical guinea pig, led his group of West-Coast followers, the Merry Pranksters, in saturnalian 'acid tests'. (Allen Ginsberg's 1965 poem, 'First Party at Ken Kesey's with Hell's Angels', records the stoned party animals' enchantment with flashing dome lights as the cop cars turn up.) Timothy Leary, a psychology professor, had researched psychedelic drugs – mainly psilocybin – at Harvard. When the university fired him in 1963 for taking his interest in them too far he turned to LSD, preaching its sacramental use through his *Psychedelic Review* and League for Spiritual Development.

Leary's slogan was 'turn on, tune in, drop out'. Both he and Kesey soon found themselves in prison, but the popularity of acid spread. The

abrupt and discordant rapid montage

enhanced consciousness and amazing visual distortion of the acid experience, together with the uncanny power of recall it conferred, was interpreted by some as the gateway to a higher reality. Fonda and Hopper had already appeared in *The Trip*, which was banned in Britain as a feature-length advertisement for LSD. But as everyone who regularly dropped acid knew, it could send you to hell as well as to heaven. The suicidal terror of the bad trip became legendary. Few who had undergone one would choose to drop acid in a cemetery.

The trip sequence, about four and a half minutes of abrupt and discordant rapid montage, ties a knot in the narrative. It is not altogether free-standing; since the murder of George Hanson, death has been creeping up. It also carries on the aesthetic logic of 'Kyrie Eleison' and the grim-sounding phrases adorning the House of Blue Lights. Hopper's 'accidents' comprise a jolting fusillade of quick-fire images that William S. Pechter, reviewing the film for *Commentary*, described as a sequence 'reprising every cliché of the genre'.

What is a cliché? The word is French for 'snapshot', and implies the mechanical, uncreative use of an expressive form. In cinema, as in writing, originality is prized; to employ clichés is to resort to stale, over-used formulations. But originality has its limits. To be as original as James Joyce means deserting a known language (in *Finnegans Wake*), not an option for popular cinema, and the very idea of genre depends on familiar repetition. Originality is always conditional on audience recognition; always a 'twist'.

In *Easy Rider* the trip montage builds a local sub-narrative, or anti-narrative, from the feverishly juxtaposed fragments of film, through an assortment of art house tricks. Critical accusations of hollow pretentiousness are close to the bone here. Nonetheless, the trip montage has its justifications.

First, as a film with an 'outlaw' profile, *Easy Rider* seeks to distance itself formally from the Hollywood tradition of reasonable, cause-and-effect narrative flow. In preferring shock and impact to fluency, it deserts the easy-reading smoothness of mainstream cinema.

Secondly, it looks to find a cinematic means of communicating the hallucinatory effects of LSD, to make the audience share them. It is virtually impossible for film to capture these warps in subjective perception optically (probably the best attempts are *2001* and *Yellow Submarine*), but *Easy Rider* strives for a filmic vocabulary that will approximate them. Hopper opts for a 'cut-up' technique, comparable to the method of the novelist William Burroughs. Also, LSD, like some other drugs, subverts the usual awareness of time. The editing of rough footage into a kaleidoscopic onslaught abolishes sequential clock time and scrambles the narrative into a rush of sensations.

These include whirlybird camera movements and oddly angled shots, vignetted shots, abstract shapes, raindrops hitting the lens, unexplained extraneous characters, inserts from the carnival parade, fuzzy and grainy textures, point-of-view tracking shots, emphatically repeated glimpses of a gloomy, decaying columbarium, light flare eclipsing the image and film stock spoiled by water, then a final fade to white before the journey is resumed. If we look at the content, we find a morbid blend of religion, death and rather desperate, joyless eroticism. On the soundtrack we hear fragments of the Creed and the Lord's Prayer, cryptic, disjointed talk and cries of distress. Mary is heard saying, 'I'm gonna die'. A biographical note intrudes when Wyatt/Fonda addresses his dead mother (at Hopper's bullying insistence, apparently).

None of this is actually meaningless, however jumbled. Images are full of meaning, like visions and altered states induced by psychedelic drugs. In fact one of the problems about the montage in the cemetery is that it is choked with meaning, as if the privileged role of chance has thrown up chaotic, excessive meaning. The incoherence of the fast-cut images may partially echo the effects of dropping acid ('imitative form'), but the frame of reference touches on big, ambitious metaphysical concerns that the film as a whole cannot seriously sustain. The visually overloaded trip sequence is a tribute to the contemporary fashion for psychedelia, though never a promotional fanfare for it.

editing

Clichéd or not, the trip sequence breaks up time, space and narrative progression. It is film as film rather than a simulacrum of reality.

editing   style

Camerawork and editing techniques are foregrounded, not invisible. But this is true to a lesser degree of the overall editing style. Hopper took a year to complete the editing with Donn Cambern, and in an interview for *Evergreen Review* he explained his method:

> I'm very given to the idea of light transmitting thought. The light-energy bouncing on the screen, the six-frame hypnotic flash hitting you, pushing you into the next scene, is better, much better, than dissolving one image over another and going out of one into another.... And I think now's not a time for that. There are no superimpositions in the film, no dissolves, we don't have time for that now – just direct-cut it.

The use of flash cuts in the release print of *Easy Rider* is comparatively modest; Hopper originally planned to plant them throughout before realising that less is more. But the omission of dissolves maximises the relatively short running-time (approximately ninety-four minutes), bypassing slow, explicit bridging or expository passages.

Some potential narrative 'waste', and a focus for critical complaint, occurs in the repeated sequences of the bikes in motion against romantically photographed landscapes. Again, Hopper had at one time envisaged a four-hour version that would dwell on what he calls 'the hypnotic feeling of movement' – inspired by the 141-minute *2001: A Space Odyssey*. In the event, cut down and underpinned by rock songs that support them thematically, these sequences don't drag. One of the great formal successes of *Easy Rider* is its linkage of songs and images to drive or modulate the narrative tempo.

Responding to the interviewer's question about the 'stanzaic structure' of the film, Hopper drew an analogy with music: 'the episodic structure, like music – something that moves along with short breaks in it'. This isn't Hopper at his most lucid, but the musical reference is apt. Music is more than an accompaniment to the rhythms of travel. It is integral with them, and the sharp cutting goes with the backbeat (see Music, below).

cinematography

The cinematographer Laszlo Kovać, a refugee from Hungary in 1956, began his mainstream Hollywood career in 1968 with Peter Bogdanovich's *Targets* and later worked on the Jack Nicholson films, *Five Easy Pieces* (1970) and *King of Marvin Gardens* (1972), as well as Hopper's *The Last Movie*. In 1976 he was one of eight cameramen filming *The Last Waltz* – the Band's final concert – for Martin Scorsese.

James Monaco, in *American Film Now*, argues that all cinematographers of the 1970s are basically realists: 'natural light is paramount, composition is fluid. It is the style of the age.' But within this bandwidth he sees Kovać, among others, as an 'expressionist', meaning that Kovać seeks images not limited to a documentary-style replication of reality. The expressive image bestows on its subject an attitude, a sentiment, a personal touch that invites the audience to respond emotionally.

In the opening scenes the predominant colours are cool blues and greys, less redolent of Mexico and Southern California than of the terse, businesslike nature of the proceedings. Many shots are close-ups, particularly of Wyatt, the 'thinking head'. The dull, steely look of the film at this stage is not exactly a promise of enjoyment. Only when Billy and Wyatt are on the road does the camera draw back to give a more colourful vista of the country they are crossing. While the editing radically compresses time, a poetic sense of time and space is created by the changing camera angles and intermittent zooms.

On the second night, in Monument Valley, the restrained use of colour is supplanted by a pan across a night sky, pink-orange-blue, with a huge sandstone mesa darkly outlined against it. As the three travellers climb the rocks in silhouette, they lose their individual features, becoming statuesque and timeless. It is a moment of absolute quiet, the most peaceful scene in the film and the most nearly 'heroic'. Equally, the lively, sparkling river glimpsed as they approach the hippy commune suggests hope and natural harmony. For the most part, though, the environment is pictured romantically but not sentimentally and usually in movement, as it is left behind. In later scenes the faded, distant look returns.

mostly he seems pretty vacant

One of the many
close-ups of Wyatt. The
framing and pose suggest
an attempt to signify
soulfulness and deep thought,
but mostly he seems
pretty vacant

subcultures developed their own uniforms

Kovaćs's versatility with the camera finds a visual register for *Easy Rider's* rhythms of feeling. Few shots – the 360° pan around the circle of solemn-faced hippies, the final soaring helicopter shot – are very long or unusual. Above all, Kovaćs's camerawork maintains the ambiguity of the quest by soberly nuancing the locations without losing a sense of excitement and wonder. Patrick McGilligan, in a survey of America's 'Ten Best' cinematographers, summarises Kovaćs's work as 'open, expansive; there is leeway and sympathy in the worst of his worlds'.

personal style: dress & appearance

One highly visible feature of the counterculture that alarmed those who saw it as anarchic and subversive was dress and appearance. From the early 1960s fashion had thrown up imaginative new styles, freeing men, especially, from the old collar-and-tie uniform to embrace more expressive forms of clothing and personal style. By 1969 fashion among the young had become extravagant, colourful and varied. Like all fashion it made a statement, defining itself against the well-groomed, straight-arrow look that had characterised the 1950s. Subcultures developed their own uniforms, and there was also plenty of scope for improvisation and individual taste – often a mix of handcrafted garments, cheap war-surplus clothing and countercultural signifiers such as peace badges.

For men, hair length became a kind of political statement. Not that long hair for men was new, as photos of nineteenth-century worthies will show. But from the early 1900s the semi-military short back and sides, or crew cut, had been the conventional masculine norm. Long hair seemed effeminate, undisciplined or rebellious. It could get you shouted at in the street – or worse. As William L. O'Neill has noted, 'once the association between beads, beards and military surplus goods on the one hand and radicalism and dope on the other, was established Middle America declared war on the counterculture's physical trappings'.

Though reviews of *Easy Rider* have often carelessly described Billy and Wyatt as hippies, they are not; the scenes at the commune confirm this.

a signifier that encodes values

Billy wears buckskin and a Western hat, bringing to mind the outlaw Billy the Kid. His hairiness is wild, almost aggressive, and matches his rough manners. Wyatt's name suggests Wyatt Earp, gunfighter and lawman, while his bike, helmet and jacket are emblazoned with the stars and stripes. Billy calls him, though he doesn't call himself, 'Captain America'. (The two characters were originally to be Captain America and Bucky, after two comic-book characters, till copyright problems intervened.)

Wyatt's flag adornments, however, can hardly be read as straightforwardly patriotic by Middle America's standards. Neither do they seem ironic or parodic in the postmodern sense. If they stand for an alternative America – freer, more tolerant and inclusive – this is barely reflected in anything he says or does. Hopper's view, or one of them, is that Wyatt is 'the Slightly Tarnished Lawman, is the sensitive, off-in-the-stars, the Great White Liberal who keeps saying, "Everything's going to work out," but... *does nothing'*. His costume is ambiguous, indeterminate, like Wyatt himself – though not to the Southern rednecks, in their baseball caps and sports shirts. They view the long hair, shades and flamboyant dress as alien and despicable, while George Hanson straddles two worlds. He wears the white suit that marks his profession, but dons a football helmet, normally the treasured memento of a college sporting career, to signify the shift in his allegiances.

Dress, then, is more than dress. It is an assertion, a signifier that encodes values and radiates meaning, above all in the visual medium of cinema.

music

Easy Rider uses music in a manner common now, but not in 1969. The rock songs are neither diegetic (emanating from a source in the narrative) nor a specially composed score (at one point Crosby, Stills and Nash were in line to provide the music, but Hopper changed his mind). They are an indispensable element of style, conjoined with the visuals. There were some precedents for this use of music, among them *The Graduate* (1967) in which Simon and Garfunkel were played over the visuals as complementary storytelling or counterpoint to them (the relevance was not always direct). In *Easy Rider* all the songs are purposefully used, both as an obvious bond of pleasure between the characters and the audience and as a formal device.

Rock 'n' roll had been born as a young people's music, a challenge to the parent generation: to its musical taste as represented by Tin Pan Alley and the standard show tune, and more deeply to a view of the world that was rooted in security, conformity and cultural conservatism. The black influence in rock 'n' roll was quickly recognised and used to attack it with tell-tale phrases like 'jungle rhythms'. But the showbiz industry began to co-opt rock 'n' roll almost at once, with contrived 'youth' movies like *Don't Knock the Rock* and the casting of Elvis in anodyne musicals. The new and exploitable youth market was addressed and the subversive energy of rock 'n' roll was refashioned as a commodity, while its stars grew rich.

Two of the numbers played early in *Easy Rider* hint that the trip across America is more than a choice: it is a destiny. These are 'Born to be Wild' by the biker's group Steppenwolf, noted for celebrating 'a cast of losers and dreamers', and 'Wasn't Born to Follow' by The Byrds, the Californian country-rock band who covered a lot of Dylan. Both convey, too, a passionate rejection of the prison of 'civilisation' and the lifeless, controlled routines of the urban herd. They are apt in every way. As well as keying in the creative influences of the heroes' generation, they supplement the theme of the search for freedom.

The third number, the Band's 'The Weight', is likewise a traveller's song. This time the weary sojourner, denied a bed, is 'lookin' for a place to hide'. The Band had backed Dylan (they can be heard on the Basement Tapes), and like Dylan's their songs tended towards a style of mythological storytelling anchored in past forms and traditional conflicts, a good match for a modern folk-tale like *Easy Rider*. 'The Weight', calling on religious imagery to picture the plight of the lone traveller, plays as they approach Monument Valley, with its legion of unseen historical ghosts.

A reprise of 'Wasn't Born to Follow' sets the mood for the hot springs scene, a hippy playground where innocent nudity and images of baptism and rebirth abound. As Billy and Wyatt head for Louisiana, where they'll drop the acid tab the Stranger gave them, the songs become acid-influenced – 'If You Want to be a Bird' by the Holy Modal Rounders,

Hendrix's 'If Six Was Nine' – and The Fraternity of Men, with 'Don't Bogart Me', supply a droll comment on George's hogging of the spliff. Additional psychedelic sounds come from The Electric Prunes and, very briefly, from The Electric Flag.

But the song of songs in *Easy Rider* is 'It's Alright, Ma (I'm Only Bleeding)' originally from the 1965 album *Bringing It All Back Home*. Dylan is already a potent subtextual presence. The Band and The Electric Flag had worked with him. The song's dense, tormented imagery indicts war, hypocrisy and consumerism and its message is bleak. Dylan, wanting an upbeat ending, at first refused permission to use it; then relented, provided Roger McGuinn sang it. And it is McGuinn who sings the film's coda, 'The Ballad of Easy Rider' over a helicopter shot that shows Wyatt's burning bike amid the lushness of wooded scenery fed by a river, a very traditional symbol of ongoing life.

There is additional, diegetic music. The hippies sing 'Let Your Hair Hang Low', with its clear resonance of countercultural freedom, and street jazz appears in the Mardi Gras sequence. All the music blends with the visual narrative, and it amply complements the two-nations theme. Billy and Wyatt ride to the sound of rock in a period of hectic, creative experimentation. The retarded and hate-crazed Southerners in the restaurant get Little Eva on the jukebox.

contexts

dimensions of context

Every film has a context – more correctly, contexts. Contexts extend as a field of meaning well beyond the specifics of a given film and the lives and work of the individuals concerned. They amount to the sum total of conditions under which a film can be made, not just a general backdrop. More: time alters and expands context, especially in relation to the viewer's experience of the text. Context is potentially infinite, but the immediate, shaping context of *Easy Rider* entails a consideration of the following:

■ The 'rules' of a given genre
Generic codes and conventions label films as catering to known pleasures and expectations: the gangster's rise and fall, SF tricks with space and time, and so forth. The codes are elastic, though. They mutate over time. They can be parodied or subverted. And there are no absolute genre boundaries; *Easy Rider* is multi-generic, as movies now increasingly tend to be.

■ Its relation to other works in the same medium
Genre study especially allows us to read one film in terms of its resemblance to others: 'intertextuality'. The self-consciousness of modern and postmodern cinema can make this virtually a precondition of enjoyment. The 'knowing' allusions to other movies in *Pulp Fiction*, for example, allow the audience to share the quotes and in-jokes which are habitually employed in contemporary cinema.

■ Its conditions of production
Easy Rider comes out of 'Hollywood', that convenient phrase for the American mainstream film industry. But Hollywood was never monolithic even in the days when eight major studios ruled the market. Since the end of the classic era it has sought to keep its pact with public taste despite

major economic change and the competition from other leisure industries. The big studios' old paternalism has gone, along with their high levels of production. What happens nowadays is the 'package': an idea, a 'treatment' and a bundle of talent in search of finance – exactly what *Easy Rider* was at its inception.

■ Its relation to larger social and political realities

It is too simple to say that films, or any other fiction, 'reflect' reality. The camera is never neutral. What we view is a partial (in both senses) version of reality. But every film reveals its broader context, however obliquely. Even when current issues are not overtly addressed, they make themselves felt. You can find 'disguised' films about Vietnam at the end of the 1960s: comedies like *M*A*S*H* (1969) or Westerns like *Soldier Blue* (1970), in which the war is a coded subtext.

Easy Rider does not take on the large public issues in the way that consciously political films do. Its blend of intimate realism, mythic beauty and archetypal conflict is not designed for airing topicalities. They are there all the same. In fact if *Easy Rider* is about anything it is about the immediate historical context that has generated the state of affairs which it epitomises – the 'coming apart' of the nation. It was a crucial moment in United States' history. But the film represents this disintegration in ways that exclude overtly political references. Hence the political context needs clarifying.

political

Easy Rider is silent on the Vietnam War. It is a loud silence. For years an outpost of the ideological Cold War, Vietnam, artificially divided into North and South, had become the theatre of an actual shooting war. The US had been intervening in South-East Asia since the Eisenhower presidency, and American ground troops had been in Vietnam since 1965, propping up a client South Vietnamese government with little support among its own people. The North Vietnamese and the Viet Cong (both North and South), fighting to reunify the country under the banner of the National Liberation Front (NLF), were perceived through Cold War eyes, and represented by American propaganda, as aggressive agents of world Communism.

political

Vietnam was a risky subject for Hollywood, as the Second World War, fought by a country united against world Fascism, had not been. The political storm centre of the decade, with dramatic repercussions on the home front, it cried out for cinematic treatment. But passions ran high, and while Americans were dying in combat with an elusive foreign enemy, any head-on treatment of the war would be more likely to divide or repel than attract the big, approving audience Hollywood sought.

There had been one attempt to sell the war as a just one. John Wayne starred in *The Green Berets* (1968), a crass and sentimental movie aimed at disproving liberal doubts about America's role. Otherwise, it remained problematic for mass-audience cinema. (The independent documentarist Emil de Antonio did make a fine, award-winning film on the history of the conflict as it stood in 1968, *In the Year of the Pig*.)

Dennis Hopper recalls being sneered at during the location filming by men who had sons in Vietnam. Yet when Billy and Wyatt talk, they discuss only either immediacies or nebulous wishes. They converse about anything but the overshadowing presence of a war that by 1969 had deeply polarised opinion and reached a critical stage. There is no indication that they watch television, read newspapers or take any interest in current affairs. They are as indifferent to the war as the film itself. Forsaking clock time for a permanent here-and-now, they are socially unattached and blind to the bigger causes to which they might relate their own push for freedom. They are apolitical and asocial.

That is to say, they are two young men who do not care about the most urgent partisan question of their time; they are self-elected exiles from the republic. If they did care, the story would be different. And there is little sign of informed opinion among the other characters, with the limited exception of George Hanson. *Easy Rider* blanks out Vietnam, by design. It is possible, all the same, for a film's 'absences' – what for one reason or another it 'forgets', sidelines, suppresses or omits – to be as instrumental in shaping its meaning as any other contextual force.

By 1969, when *Easy Rider* was released, Vietnam had become a major fault line in American public opinion. Despite the barrage of official news that depicted the war as a struggle for freedom and democracy against a ruthless and fanatical enemy, support for it was ebbing. The North Vietnamese port of Hanoi remained open during the war, and the international media operated outside the control of US military censorship. Too many reports from the battlefield contradicted the State Department line. Young men of military age increasingly refused the draft.

Graver still, at the start of 1968 the myth of American invincibility was shattered by the Tet Offensive against South Vietnamese cities. Territory taken by the Viet Cong was won back, but its successes shook the American war machine in Vietnam. As the footage of events which were never supposed to happen was screened in American living rooms, it undermined belief at home in the empty promises of victory.

1968

The year 1968 was one of seismic sensations, not only in America. But wherever they took place, America was an ideological presence. It had become two nations, America and 'Amerika' (a spelling adopted by the New Left and counterculture to suggest a parallel between American policy and Nazism – aggression abroad, repression at home), as opposed attitudes and convictions crystallised around the war, racial difference, lifestyle and political moralities. On 31 March 1968, President Johnson announced he would not be standing for re-election. Senator Eugene McCarthy had already declared his intention to run as a peace candidate, against the Democratic Party machine. Later – too late – Robert Kennedy entered the race for the Democratic nomination. Outside regular politics, violence spoke: Martin Luther King, Jr was assassinated in April, sparking off black upheavals, Robert Kennedy was shot and killed in June.

In the summer of 1968 the Democratic National Convention in Chicago was the scene of a brutal and panicky police riot. The Chicago force was let loose on McCarthy supporters, anti-war protesters and the 'Yippies' (the Youth International Party), who attended in a spirit of subversive fun. Hubert Humphrey, the pro-war candidate, was nominated in a poisoned atmosphere.

Divisions sprang up, and divisions within divisions, as the policymakers privately agreed they could not win in Vietnam while the New Left peaked, then split into quarrelling factions and marginal groups. As always, there were rewards to be won from turmoil. The main beneficiary was the Republican presidential candidate Richard Nixon, once a discredited figure from the past. He was elected in November, defeating Humphrey, Johnson's vice-president, on a promise to end the war and reunite the nation. On the stump, he liked to quote the slogan he had read on a placard held up by a child: 'Bring Us Together'.

This, in brief, is the shaping political context of *Easy Rider*, invisible and unheard on the screen but epitomised by the culture clash it represents – the meeting of two worlds, both American but speaking different languages. It is a standoff. The film has no more power to resolve the differences than Nixon's rhetoric, and pushes them to a violent, uncompromising outcome. Yet *Easy Rider* tells nothing of the war itself; of the national debate around it; of the struggles continuing in the streets and on college campuses; of the outgroups, such as the blacks, who had linked the anti-war movement to their own fight for freedom; of concerted resistance to the draft; of coverage in the media. These are there as shadows and echoes in the film's ideological concerns.

ideological

Ideology is a vital but awkward concept. It refers to beliefs, attitudes and opinions – conscious or not – reproduced in society (through the family, education, the media and so on) and 'lived' by individuals as if they were natural, or objectively real. Capitalism, Communism, Christianity and Democracy are all ideologies. There are racist and sexist ideologies, ideologies of art and science. There are also counter-ideologies of resistance and protest. In film and other media, ideology takes the form of representations: fictional versions of the real world. Giving the illusion of reality, they stand for only a 'spun' version of reality, unavoidably biased or incomplete. Even so, these representations may be graphically convincing if they answer a need in the audience, or support its preconceptions.

To take an example: in Hollywood films of the 1930s and 1940s, black people rarely appear. When they do, they play small, lower-order parts, often rolling their eyes and behaving foolishly or superstitiously. By the

precursors of the alternative society

1960s things have changed. Sidney Poitier has become a pioneering black star. The grossest racist impersonations have gone. Stereotyping has not disappeared, and the most favoured black characters have essentially white liberal values, but for the most part sympathetic tolerance has supplanted hostile derision. This change certainly owes much to the mobilisation of blacks in the Civil Rights Movement (to secure full rights for themselves in the 1950s and 1960s), but what it is most directly symptomatic of is a shift in the viewpoint of white ideology. Hollywood can no longer count on there being an audience that automatically dismisses black Americans as comically stupid maids and shoeshine boys.

Representations, then, are ideological products that 'encode' the real. That does not mean that they are pure propaganda with a single message (though *The Green Berets* came close). As a rule, ideology works through what is taken for granted – hidden assumptions – rather than by what is expressly stated. Hollywood films normally operate within a liberal/conservative ideology, not out to change the social and economic system from which they draw their profits but seldom élitist or authoritarian. Often the keynote is 'populism', a celebration of the virtues of ordinary and humble but democratically minded people.

But audiences shift, change and subdivide. From the 1950s onwards, the youth market bloomed. With typical opportunism Hollywood responded to this market, and the uneasy sense of a 'generation gap', with 'youth movies'. It was in this decade that the distinctive 'rebel males' of modern American cinema – principally Marlon Brando and James Dean – made their greatest impact. Brando and Dean represented misunderstood youth in confused revolt in movies like *The Wild One* (1953), *East of Eden* (1955) and *Rebel Without a Cause* (1955). Here there was an ideological standoff between the films' narrative urge to win disaffected youth over to civic and family values and the stars' 'charismatic' images of provocative defiance.

In these films liberalism shows in the preference for understanding and sympathy rather than punishment, and the critique of poor parenting; conservatism in the closure that redeems the hero in order to integrate him into society. But Brando and Dean were still precursors of the alternative society of the 1960s. Their mystique exceeded the constraints of their screen roles. They were icons who promised the advent of alternative values, of teenagers and young adults who were not just mixed up and in need of straightening out but had anti-establishment agendas of their own. Though their film roles reconciled them with the prevailing ideological formation they were harbingers of eruptive new ideological forces, which by the late 1960s were winning adherents and making headlines.

A 'SIXTIES' IDEOLOGY'?

It is impossible to write of a single 1960s' ideology, one that would accommodate everything from fashion to politics. 'Swinging' is a limp and inadequate term. 'Sex, drugs and rock 'n' roll' provided major interests and pleasures, but there was no absolute uniformity of outlook even among those who enjoyed them. The New Left in America was energetic and vocal, but its attitudinising and its own internal disputes led David Zane Mairowitz to christen it 'the radical soap opera'. I was once told by a student who must have been born around 1968 that the 1960s were 'all red tee-shirts and fists in the air'; but there were as many dropouts as activists: there were hippies who wanted to till the land, radicals who organised in the cities, artists, self-publicists, bullshitters and those who just wanted to smoke dope and play sounds in their spare time. (And there were straights who carried on as before.) The strength and weakness of the 1960s' dynamic was that it was open and non-doctrinaire, 'demanding the impossible' with no agreed programme.

What it did have was a free commitment to experimentation and newness, even when it dug into the past for ideas and style tips. And now that the decade has hardened into myth as an ideological club wielded by both sides to condemn or justify what has happened since, it is impossible to recover a final truth about it. But it is worth quoting the immediate verdict, in 1971, of a high-profile countercultural author, the 'gonzo journalist' Hunter S. Thompson. Meditating on the lost dream in *Fear and Loathing in Las Vegas*, he wrote:

> History is hard to know, because of all the hired bullshit, but even
> without being sure of 'history' it seems entirely reasonable to
> think that every now and then the energy of a whole generation

> comes to a head in a long fine flash, for reasons that nobody
> understands at the time – and which never explain, in retrospect,
> what actually happened.

You could hardly call that non-ideological. It is too nostalgic (already) to be a detached judgement, though it is not uncritical. The metaphor of 'a long, fine flash', both diffuse and concentrated, implies it could never have lasted. But in many ways the youth movement of the 1960s was a flash – not a full consensus, not a unanimous cause or an agreed manifesto, more a shared feeling of liberation from constricting taboos.

Partly for this reason, it could not be automatically adapted to established Hollywood formulae. Hollywood was hardly a young institution and it had to consider the silent majority for whom the new youth subcultures were a symptom of anarchy and subversion. Among the first films to tackle them honestly were documentaries from the independent sector, like *Monterey Pop* (1968) and *Woodstock* (1970). The Woodstock Festival (originally promoted as a 'music and arts fair') in 1969 featured gestural nudity, prolific drug consumption and the music that was the excuse for the whole thing. Even there, white middle-class youth seemed to predominate, and not all the songs were as rousingly political as Country Joe Macdonald's version of 'Fixin' to Die'.

Such films broke the old Hollywood mould for rock 'n' roll, which had contained it with beach parties and high-school hops. By 1969 rock was a wide-scale cultural intervention, far more than a spare-time interest. It came from below, created by the young from their own experience and desires, even if it was then processed through the recording and concert industry. Like Vietnam ('the first rock 'n' roll war') rock music had acquired a militant edge. Its ideology, as its name suggested, was not amenable to law and order. Rock documentaries showed the counterculture at play, dancing and grooving to the music, pursuing self-expression. Their value as eye-witness records is indisputable, even when the concert is the pretext for the film.

Far more of a challenge was accommodating rock culture into feature films, in which fundamental conflicts needed to be smoothed by closure; but the music, and the tempo of cultural militancy, grew more insistent.

cultural & cinematic

Hollywood had been reshaping itself since the postwar dissolution of the vertically integrated major studio system. It had had to compete with television and other rival leisure sources. Audience profiles had altered as the average age of cinema-goers went down, and ambitious new stars were making their names. The restrictive Production Code, the industry's self-censorship apparatus, had been progressively relaxed from the 1950s, so that movies could be more grown up, less coy, on matters like sex, than the bland family fare of TV. Doris Day's career as a virgin tease was petering out as she moved from feature films to advertising margarine on the small screen. Established genres continued, but the pressure for novelty often redrafted their conventions. Films from Europe and further abroad were creeping out of the art house ghetto; Jean-Luc Godard of the French *nouvelle vague* ('new wave'), for example, took Hollywood pulp material, turned it around, and fed it back to American cinema as a reviving tonic.

Within the industry independent producers moved into positions of influence. Roger Corman, for one, had been producing and directing cheap, profitable B pictures since the mid-1950s. The titles give some idea of the Corman touch – *Swamp Women, It Conquered the World, Attack of the Crab Monsters* – but as David Thomson writes in his *A Biographical Dictionary of the Cinema*:

> Corman seized what was a dying form, re-established its worth, and managed to introduce its crazy disciplines to the indulgent perceptions of underground cinema. Few contemporary directors have set such a vigorous example to young, imaginative people yearning to make movies....

Hopper, Fonda and Nicholson had all worked with Corman and learnt from his approach. They had also been immersed in subcultures that extended beyond the Hollywood industry, hanging out with artists, writers and alternative personalities in the ferment of 1960s' iconoclasm. In a milieu where mainstream movie-making, hard business, artistic aspiration, radical ideas and the pursuit of pleasure all intermingled, the old divide between commercial movies and the art or independent film was little respected. The energetic cross-currents of the 1960s pushed confidently at traditional boundaries.

There had been earlier signs and portents in the cultural front. Among the few disruptive elements of what the poet Robert Lowell called 'the tranquillised fifties' were the Beat writers: principally Jack Kerouac, Allen Ginsberg and Gregory Corso. Kerouac's *On the Road* (1957) celebrated, rather like *Easy Rider*, spontaneous movement for its own sake, or for the sake of 'freedom'. It was written in a virtually unedited rush of words, designed to capture the pure sensation of the moment. Ginsberg had published a long poem of anguish and accusation, *Howl*, in 1955.

Ginsberg had survival value. He went on to become an almost ever-present 1960s' figure, loved by the media, as he graced high-profile countercultural events with his mix of protest, humour and Eastern mysticism. Ken Kesey brought out his novel *One Flew Over the Cuckoo's Nest*, in 1962. Its hero, Randle McMurphy, is a free spirit locked up in a mental ward, and the symbolic lesson was obvious: like the Soviet Union, America treated its dissidents as mental cases. The book became a cult (and later a film starring Jack Nicholson); few noticed at the time the novel's ingrown misogyny.

There were new currents flowing in cinema, too. John Cassavetes used his earnings from TV and Hollywood parts to help finance personal films, starting with *Shadows* (1961). Though not exactly underground cinema, these films had limited releases, and *Shadows* was his one real success. They were marked by a rejection of Hollywood gloss and a preference for taut, intimate situations rather than expansive drama or action. Cassavetes's techniques included actor improvisation, hand-held camerawork, choppy editing and the overall feel of documentary. If his work now looks dull and earnest, it did begin to erode the distinction between mass-audience and independent cinema.

Of the new generation of directors, the future maestro Martin Scorsese was still a film student at New York University in the early 1960s. His first feature film *Who's That Knocking at My Door?* was released in 1969 (though initiated much earlier). He worked on *Woodstock* as assistant director and editor and then directed the gang picture *Boxcar Bertha* (1972) for Roger Corman. With Corman, as David Thompson notes in *Scorsese on Scorsese*, he found 'the freedom to test his radical, aesthetic ambitions against the discipline of genre imperatives and audience reaction'.

These words could almost be applied to *Easy Rider*. It is precisely at a time of intense polarisation in America – social, political, cultural, ethnic – that alternative visions of both cinema and reality discover the will and opportunity to revise the cultural agenda. For Hollywood, the youth audience was a big potential market that it could not rely on tapping through its traditional mindset and working practices. That meant admitting fresh ideas. To those on the other side of the divide, film was a unique means of reaching others who might share their dissatisfactions and their hopes. Out of this came what Richard Martin, in *Mean Streets, Raging Bulls*, calls 'the fusion of mainstream and art cinema film-making techniques in the *nouvelle vague*-influenced Hollywood renaissance cinema of the late sixties and early seventies'. *Easy Rider* has the deserved status of a forerunner.

industrial

Not that American cinema was fully radicalised. Just as you will find plenty of corny ballads and novelty songs among the chart hits of the 1960s, traditional movie genres continued alongside the burgeoning of the New Hollywood. They benefited from the relaxation of film censorship, though as usual not all were profitable despite the basic safety-first policy of the leading production companies. The reliance on tried and trusted factors – 'timeless' genres, big stars, family fare, formulaic sex and violence – shows up in other releases of 1969 such as *Paint Your Wagon* (originally a 1951 stage musical), *The Wild Bunch* (a macho Peckinpah Western with Vietnam echoes), *Hello Dolly!* (a Streisand flop), *Butch Cassidy and the Sundance Kid* (Paul Newman and Robert Redford as buddies). The following year a dismal romantic weepie, *Love Story*, was a smash hit.

Flux was the key. Columbia had been one of the cheap outfits in the years of classic Hollywood. In the late 1960s it was a hidebound, conservative company keen to exploit the youth market but at a frustrating distance from it. Nonetheless, it was the release company for *Easy Rider*. A look at the production history of *Easy Rider* unveils the complex of interests that enabled an unexpected hit such as *Easy Rider* to be made. Because *Easy Rider's* story hinged on the adventures of two cocaine dealers who are sympathetically represented, it was a tricky project to finance, but, though planned as a low-budget feature on the Corman model, with cast and crew working for scale, it still needed backers. Negotiations with AIP proved fruitless. Corman initially approved and agreed to act as a producer, but Sam Arkoff and Jim Nicholson, in charge at AIP, asked for conditions which Fonda and Hopper felt would compromise their independence. In early 1968, prompted by Jack Nicholson, they pitched their idea to Bob Rafelson and Ray Schneider at Raybert Productions.

Raybert had prospered, in large measure, thanks to The Monkees, a manufactured group of four moptops whose quirky escapades and catchy songs proved popular in television and for whom Jack Nicholson had scripted the follow-up movie *Head*. It was committed to funding talent by providing capital, then letting the film-makers alone – the opposite of the old 'producer control' system of classic Hollywood. Fonda and Hopper were granted the $360,000 they asked for and were to receive a third of the take, with Bert Schneider filling the role of executive producer.

Raybert's unorthodox, progressive strategy favoured an auteur cinema, with the film-makers given control. This meant that Fonda, as producer, did not have accountants on his back during the shooting, and was free to contend with Dennis Hopper's ego. The deal was concluded with the recruitment of Terry Southern. According to Fonda, the final cost of *Easy Rider* was $500,000. Schneider had close family connections with Columbia and could arrange the release.

At one level it is easy to see how it all worked. Corman had shown what could be done to mix *shlock* with artistry in movies that drew young, cultish audiences. By the late 1960s, it appeared that cheap biker movies and cheap druggie movies could make big money; *Easy Rider* is both. Mass identification with the counterculture meant that new archetypes and new stars were needed in youth-oriented films that were not moralistic, bogus, patronising or just dead on the screen. *Easy Rider* found a ready market.

At the same time, *Easy Rider* illustrates 'the genius of the system'. Despite its overall commitment to the status quo and the mass market, Hollywood as a source of popular cultural products has always been innovative and versatile. That is its history from the start. In many ways it is a wasteful industry – some of its losses have been breathtaking – but it is also an adaptable one. Social and economic change since the Second World War had restructured it but had not destroyed its driving spirit – to make films, nearly always with some regard for quality, and make money. *Easy Rider* emerged from a collaboration of different personnel, motives and interests. It could not have been successfully made without the input of new talent, but among the complex of aesthetic and commercial forces that drove Hollywood were backers prepared to trust and promote that talent. It was a smart move. *Easy Rider* became *the* road movie, the benchmark of a genre.

road movies

At one time a *Road* movie meant Bob Hope and Bing Crosby gagging their way through a comedy script set in some exotic, though studio-built, location. *The Road to...* series ran for over twenty years; the last, *Road to Hong Kong*, appeared in 1962. Foreign travel was the cinematic excuse for safe, low-grade comedy.

There had been other, more serious films focusing on automobile treks across America. *The Grapes of Wrath* (1939) had pictured an historic forced migration, out of economic necessity. Several *films noirs* feature the 'young couple on the run'. The car itself, like the horse in Westerns, was already an archetypal character in Hollywood cinema, not an incidental. As Eric Mottram notes in an essay on cars in American films, cars in movies 'are used for other purposes besides transport'. They become signifiers of personality, status or attitude. Brand names matter.

Plenty of movies can be thought of as road movies, as the variety of unalike films collected in Mark Williams's *Road Movies* demonstrates. But in the type of modern road movie most relevant to *Easy Rider* we find elective

Hell's Angels had no time for peace

movement, an existential quest – for the self, for America – that is simultaneously a flight. Whatever the ostensible reason for the journey, it embodies the drive to create meaning and identity in an 'absurd' world. The alienated suicide runs of *Vanishing Point* and *Two Lane Blacktop* (both 1971) and the unrelenting chase in Steven Spielberg's début movie *Duel* (1972) take urban paranoia on to the broad highway. In *Badlands* (1973, but set fifteen years earlier) the fugitive young couple reappear, trapped by the violent impulses of their society as their stolen Cadillac takes them through the natural splendours of the northern Midwest.

biker movies

In *Easy Rider* two men who apparently have a perfectly good pickup truck choose to cross a continent on customised motorcycles which scare people and have minimal luggage space. It is the sacrifice of good sense and practical advantage to an icon. And in the 1960s the iconic bike (above all the Harley Davidson) was associated with biker gangs and Hell's Angels. Social undesirables to straight America, Hell's Angels had no time for peace and love either. Many were only too eager to fight in Vietnam (criminal pasts tended to prevent them). Their anarchic descent on a small Californian town, Bass Lake, in 1965 had echoed the plot of *The Wild One*. It was chronicled by Hunter S. Thompson in *Hell's Angels* (1966). Bikes were linked with men who styled themselves 'outlaws'. The heavy-duty bike acquired connotations of wildness and freedom beyond the relatively small membership circles of biker gangs.

Cinematically, the Angels took to the roads *en masse* in the 1960s. The catalyst was Corman's *The Wild Angels* (1966). Like *Easy Rider*, this was an official entry at a major European festival (Venice). Thanks to its exciting 'scenes of gang rape… and endless drug and alcohol abuse' (Mark Williams) it was feared and loathed by civic-minded Middle America but a magnet for the young male audience, and it set a trend. *Born Losers* and *Devil's Angels* were quickly made and released the following year. *Angels from Hell* appeared in 1968 (its hero a disillusioned Vietnam veteran); *Hell's Angels* in 1969; *The Losers* in 1970. *Angels Hard as They Come* ((1971) gave Jonathan Demme his first chance at directing a feature film.

Low production values, hackneyed dialogue and barely adequate acting could be expected in cheap biker-gang movies. Lashings of raw sex and violence helped sell them. Billy and Wyatt do not share that, any more than they do the gang ethos. But the iconic bike as the twentieth-century horse, carrying its rider away from the static corruption of role-conditioned obedience, evokes the savour that the biker exploitation pictures also have of adventure, mobility and the great outdoors.

social representations

Students of literature, film and other disciplines now commonly employ the analytical triad of class, race and gender to explore the ideology of a given book or movie. This is a more sophisticated way of understanding texts than the old trinity of character, theme and plot. It does not mean hunting down and denouncing the oppressive bias of the author (commonly an all too simple task), only finding a better developed objective context for relating fiction to the real, social world.

The erasure in *Easy Rider* of any concrete sociopolitical reference has already been noted. Its model is the traditional American search for individual freedom, not a call to reform society. But the point about the concepts of class, race and gender is that they can be used to highlight the political nature of personal relations and everyday actions – not through what characters say necessarily, but through the assumptions they, or the author, habitually make. Like any text, *Easy Rider* reveals those assumptions as much by what it neglects and takes for granted, or 'naturalises', as by what it consciously expresses.

The most glaring example, from the safe distance of thirty years, is its representation of women. They have a subordinate role in the narrative and the credits for understandable reasons: this is a film about male experience. Male-centredness in an art work does not have to be sexist. But where women make few appearances, it is worth asking how they are represented when they do appear. The answer here seems to be: mainly in stereotypical roles – mothers and homemakers, gossipy teen queens, prostitutes. *Easy Rider* does not mock or abuse these women, any more than it represents its heroes as masterful, superior males. They are just the chauvinism of 'Pig Amerika'

women doing what women do, and women do not take off across the country on bikes. Women, in short, are not conceived of as existential beings, rather as fixed, essential ones.

GENDER

The struggles of the 1960s created temporary coalitions of protest and resistance among groups who otherwise often had separate interests. Blacks, drafted in disproportionate numbers, rallied against the war, annexing it to racism at home; but there was much they did not have in common with white radicals. Student protesters could appear as play-acting middle-class malcontents to ill-paid workers. And women were challenging not only the chauvinism of 'Pig Amerika' but a male-centred idea of revolution which treated them as a support group available for sex, cookery and rolling the joints. (The black activist Stokeley Carmichael once famously declared that 'the only position for women [in our movement] is prone'.) By the end of the 1960s second-wave feminism was adding its own incisive arguments to the agenda of change. The backlash was fast and virulent. William L. O'Neill has graphically recorded the horror, hatred and ridicule that the women's liberation movement of the 1960s faced from its inception:

> The violent abuse that feminists everywhere encountered was all out of proportion to what they did. Liberal men like David Susskind invited them on television for the sole purpose of insulting them, so it seemed. Everyone with the slightest experience in these matters was struck by how much sheer bigotry men (and brainwashed women too) were willing to express. In fact, among ordinary middle-class people anti-feminism seemed the only remaining respectable prejudice. It was once socially acceptable to hate Jews, Negroes, immigrants, and the like. That was no longer true.... Only the hatred of women (and homosexuals) remained.

Mocking and scornful objections to the 'libbers' were heard from men who ought to have known better, like Norman Mailer, as the women's movement exposed the bedrock conservatism of many anti-establishment males. As O'Neill points out, 'One reason feminism was always taken lightly was that to take it seriously opened up dreadful possibilities' – of demolishing male privilege and power, of upsetting the family and marriage system that gave men authority.

The women's movement was already developing its own stars, whose polemics struck a chord with thousands of their sisters. Betty Friedan had published *The Feminine Mystique* in 1963. Out of it developed the National Organisation of Women (NOW), a countrywide pressure group. Anne Koedt's influential essay *The Myth of the Vaginal Orgasm* first appeared as a radical feminist pamphlet, one of many aimed at male suprematism. Frighteningly, it implied that men were unnecessary to women's sexual pleasure. By the end of the decade women's groups were fast building their strength in forums like SDS (Students for a Democratic Society – the active original core of the New Left), and Kate Millett had published *Sexual Politics* (1968), which included a critical rereading of admired male authors, Mailer among them. Second-wave feminism, unlike some other ideological offshoots of the time, had come to stay. Though it never spoke with a single voice, the women's movement proved its strength by the opposition it stirred up.

There is scarcely a hint of this in *Easy Rider*, which appears a shade too early to recognise and respond to a potent surge of ideas and activism that would shake the ruling ideology. The omission betrays both a central flaw in the fast-splitting counterculture and New Left – their one-eyed view of liberation – and the slowness of Hollywood to engage with serious new social interventions. (Hollywood did catch up, eventually. By 1975 Scorsese, the chronicler of male peer groups in *Mean Streets*, felt the need to address gender issues in *Alice Doesn't Live Here Any More* – and employ women crew members).

Women are subordinate in the film while they were actually fighting the nervous assaults of unreconstructed masculinity, no longer suppressed or coaxed into silence in the national dialogue. *Easy Rider* demonstrates a lack of interest in women and feminism more than misogyny, and indeed a minimal interest in sex, which appears much less of a lure to Billy and

Wyatt than drugs and rock 'n' roll. The classic Western, in which a secondary love interest is often stuck on to a tale of men being men, seems almost erotic by comparison.

RACE

Easy Rider sidelines both women and feminism. Not so with race, though it is scarcely at the centre. From the 1950s the Civil Rights Movement, under the aegis of non-violent leaders like Martin Luther King, Jr, had pushed for equality. It had ended legal segregation in the South and prompted the federal government to enact important civil rights legislation in 1964. By the 1960s it was neither liberal nor hip to see blacks as inferior, though racism was far from extinct. George Hanson makes the point crisply when he tells his new buddies that they'll be freed provided they've not killed 'anyone white'. Also he has worked with the ACLU (the American Civil Liberties Union), which involved itself with civil rights cases. And the 'rural witticisms' of the men in the restaurant – the enemy – draw on hard-core racist abuse (coupling it with homophobia). *Easy Rider* is implicitly 'right on' where race is concerned.

But only implicitly. Black people are scarce in the film, seen by the roadside, living in shacks that contrast with the great plantation houses, extras in the carnival parade in New Orleans, voices on the soundtrack. Blacks were culture heroes, creative and streetwise, to many young hipsters. *Easy Rider* marginalises them, mirroring their history as a marginalised people in WASP (White Anglo-Saxon Protestant)-dominated America, but not their resistance to it.

There are, however, Mexicans in the opening sequence. It is quite usual for Mexico to be pictured as a hell of squalor, criminality, violence and death, outlaw territory, in American films (for an extreme case see *Bring Me the Head of Alfredo Garcia*). But in *Easy Rider*, though the cocaine deal is illegal, Mexico appears as a genial, relaxed place ('Contenta'). Something approaching a blood brotherhood seems to flourish between Jesús and Wyatt. The camera takes time to dwell on the weatherbeaten faces of Jesús's *compadres*, using the steady, affirmative, full-face portraiture that is a photographic code for dignity. They may be bystanders with no lines to speak; they are not the threatening or wheedling Latinos of the Anglo stereotype.

CLASS

To discuss *Easy Rider* (or almost any American film) in terms of class is difficult. Classes in the United States, though they certainly exist, lack the clear and obvious cultural profiles we are used to in Britain. Other inequalities are more to the foreground, and speech, the giveaway in England, is often regionally rather than class inflected. But it is worth noting that Billy and Wyatt are differentiated by, among other things, some surface indicators of class. Wyatt has the sensitive face and diffident manners of a well-bred college boy. Billy is more blue-collar in his looks, speech and behaviour. George Hanson is clearly middle class, by occupation, while the white-trash bigots probably belong to the rural working or lower-middle class, whose social allegiance is very localised. However, the film is not governed by any central class ideology. Its focus is generational and existential.

If I had to fix an ideological label on *Easy Rider* it would be 'permissive'. Applied to the overthrow of sexual and other taboos in the 1960s, it became a word unappetising to straights and alternatives alike: by one side because they felt it licensed falling standards, by the other because they considered their freedoms to be rights for which no permission was needed. The word lost its original shine as it was worn down to a stale media tag.

Yet it does mean something. More concretely in this instance, it fits a notion of freedom derived from the historical experience of a nation that created itself out of the hazardous colonisation of a huge territory. The doctrine of individual rights and the vision of endless horizons placed a special cachet on the right to be left alone to wander at will, free from the interference of government and society. Billy and Wyatt are harmless, except in the fantasies of bottom-feeding rednecks. They are quite ordinary young men under the fancy dress, drifters whose background is as trick riders at rodeos and carnivals (Billy alludes to this boastfully when they are jailed). They have no sense of society and are no use to it.

But it is impossible to think of them as the bad guys. If they are social undesirables from Middle America's point of view they are doing no harm. They are not killing other men, in Vietnam or anywhere else; quite the contrary. Neither are they attempting to stop the killing; the peace movement holds no interest for them. Permissiveness and wanderlust have no chance of changing the world. The journey is an escape, a suspension of time. Unfortunately, to hope to escape the turbulent upheavals and fierce pressures of America at the end of the 1960s is really to demand the impossible.

DRUGS

Except in the minds of tabloid editors and some politicians, drugs are no longer hugely sensational. A thriving underground economy feeds demand. The widespread use of recreational drugs, especially cannabis and cocaine, is a fact; at the same time prohibition is backed by a costly and futile 'war on drugs'. While illegal, drug consumption cannot be completely normalised, but it is one of the discoveries of the 1960s that has continued and spread.

Naturally, not everyone used drugs in the 1960s and not all those who did had the same motive. A sacramental approach, like Leary's to LSD, went with the religious yearnings of the decade, its proto-New Age facets. One critique of American society, and far from a new one, was that it had become despiritualised through its obsessive pursuit of wealth and power and the prodigious attractions of its consumer economy. For some users, altered states promised a transcendence of gross materialism. Others had hedonistic motives: getting high, tripping out. Cannabis made a sympathetic trio with sex and rock 'n' roll. Speed kept you awake, so you didn't have to miss any of the fun. Psychedelics brought amazing visions and blended the senses. The scale of consumption meant that inflexible laws criminalised millions of young Americans.

Many rock groups embraced the widening drug culture and wove the experience into their music, strengthening the bond with their audiences. Todd Gitlin recalls the dope scene in his subjective and personal memoir *The Sixties: Years of Hope, Days of Rage:*

> we would sit around listening, awed, all sensation, to Dylan's or
> somebody else's images bursting out of one another like Roman
> candles... the afternoons and evenings seeming to stretch, the
> present liquidly filling all time past and time future, not just the
> words but the spaces between notes saturated by significance,
> the instruments sounding in the ear more distinctly than could
> have been imagined before.

Drugs were already associated with establishment bugbears – black people,
jazz, criminality, orgies, UnAmericanism, otherness – and classic Hollywood
cinema, under the heavy constraints of the Production Code, had held
them at arm's length. The idiotic *Reefer Madness* (1936) now circulates on
video as a smoker's camp cult item. Later, less hysterical films stressed drug
use – or rather addiction – as a problem, deriving from, and causing, other
problems. *The Man with the Golden Arm* (1955) was a pitiless study of
smack as the Devil.

Twelve years later the outrage provoked by *The Trip* suggested that, though
the American cinema's representations of drug use were finally shifting, it
was still capable of inspiring a moral panic. In a sense, an alarmed reaction
was merited. Not because acid meant madness and breakdown, but
because the underground pleasures of it and other drugs broke a major
taboo, and frequently went with a similar attitude to other conventional
obligations, such as nine-to-five work, official morality and civil obedience.
The anti-narcotics laws brought the law into disrepute and encouraged the
organised crime initiatives that preyed on the user.

Inevitably there were those, headliners and others, who embraced the
pleasure principle to their own cost. Many more, like Billy and Wyatt, made
cannabis a comfortable part of their way of life; dope as an enhancement
of everyday living, not a pathway to Nirvana. The smoking scenes in *Easy
Rider* provide some of its happiest moments. It is not given any special
mystique, but the ritual, and the mellowing effect, induce a temporary
good humour and relaxation, a respite from the long, dusty road.

LAW & ORDER

Richard Nixon ran a prudent and evasive presidential campaign in 1968,
vague on practical solutions. Suicidal disunity in the Democratic Party won

'Law and order' ... a weasel phrase

the presidency for him – just. But in his speeches he never forgot to press the law-and-order button when he was sure it would rouse his audience. In the election, he shared the south with a third-party candidate, the law-and-order 'ultra', George Wallace of Alabama, who took five states including Louisiana.

'Law and order' is a weasel phrase. In principle, few would argue with its logic. The safety of citizens and their property should be guaranteed by the state, most agree. But in practice during the 1960s it became a cipher for the repression of dissent and protest. In particular, it stood for the primitive wish of the frightened silent majority to punish outgroups who would not go quietly – students, hippies, blacks, countercultural types, feminists. This backlash was effortlessly exploited by conservative politicians. It also licensed the aggression of an increasingly militarised police, as at the 1968 Democratic National Convention. Two years later, panicky National Guardsmen shot dead four demonstrating students at Kent State University, Ohio, injuring many others. Black Panthers were gunned down by police officers. The extreme response, as in Vietnam, tended to be the first response.

In other words, law and order as a maxim, like anti-Communism, became the pretext for lawless violence and brutality on the part of the authorities, and of individuals. This urge was reflected, too, in legislation that amplified police powers. Middle America, as Nixon well understood, was happy to see freaks and protesters robbed of their civil liberties. Not that most law-abiding citizens were personally keen to use guns, or even hair clippers. They generally left that to the police and the army.

But the potential for violence was omnipresent. Some rogue elements of the New Left, like the Weathermen, actively sought it and paid with cracked skulls and crippling lawsuits. Yet it wasn't necessary to be a confrontationist to disturb the silent majority; the odium of long hair could be enough, certainly in the most 'primitive' parts of the nation. *Easy Rider* takes its heroes through the hostile environment of the deep South, and the South is different. There the Stars and Stripes can be considered the flag of an invader, as a casual comment in the restaurant scene illustrates.

The South's diehard attitudes entailed, more than elsewhere, a tough line on dissidents. Law and order in Dixie had once meant keeping the blacks down. It had fought the Civil Rights Movement and lost. In *Easy Rider* it substitutes for its historic racism an ingrained and murderous intolerance of hipster freaks – 'white Negroes', to borrow Mailer's coinage (not that Billy shows any respect for 'weirdo hicks'). 'You name it, I'll throw rocks at it' is the knee-jerk law-and-order reaction to longhairs.

There is a genuine historical basis to the abrupt Southern vigilante violence that kills Billy and Wyatt. The historical record of lynchings and other vicious punishments is horrifying. You could still say the South is unfairly represented in *Easy Rider*; there was plenty of blind repression elsewhere. The cruelty, fanaticism and bitterness of the Vietnam syndrome came home with a vengeance across America.

But just as Billy and Wyatt are an extreme case of dropping out to do your own thing, so the redneck sheriff and the casually homicidal duckhunters typify the law and order mania at its most terrifying, ignorant and savage. A national conflict is signified through a heightened local conflict.

Thanks to its intensive and concentrated representation of the chasm of mutual distrust between Middle America and the counterculture, *Easy Rider* survives as a dramatisation of profound social rifts. If the film is a fantasy, it is what Raymond Chandler called 'a fantasy of the possible'. What is shown in the fiction *could* happen. The South had proved during the Freedom Rides of the 1960s that it was prepared to kill outsiders. Often law officers were implicated, either directly or through a cover-up.

But the South only exaggerated a national taste for violence. Under Johnson and Nixon the B52s rained death and destruction on Vietnam. At home, police were quick on the draw with nightsticks and gas. Left fringe groups were making bombs. Blacks, exploited and fobbed off, tore down their ghettoes. The debate had gone beyond words. The final catastrophe of *Easy Rider* is a plausible ending which writes up a farewell to 1960s' optimism in its final, receding image for the expiration of the dream – thousands of dollars in a blazing gas tank.

audiences

There is a simple test for judging a movie's attractiveness to film-goers: the box office. Sybil Delgaudio reports that '*Easy Rider* ... became Columbia's fourth highest grossing movie of the 1960s, and by 1991 had earned over $19 million.' Promotional campaigns, press reviews and word of mouth all play their part in building a movie's reputation. In the end, the public decides. But to know that a film succeeded commercially is not the same as knowing what meanings the audience took from it. The mass audience that Hollywood has mostly sought was never a single audience, and has increasingly fragmented. This is recognised now in the targeting of niche audiences. *Easy Rider* itself was a response to the recognition that a young audience could be drawn to films that sympathetically represented its own mores and interests.

Film-goers react individually to what they see on the screen, but they are not empty vessels. Inevitably, their taste will be conditioned – by age, class, race and gender as well as by personal inclination. *Easy Rider* is aimed at youth, mainly at urban male youth. It is hard to believe that it ever had the same appeal for female viewers as it did for men, or that middle-aged Southern duckhunters admired it. And it is not necessary to believe that of those who did see and enjoy *Easy Rider*, all thought it was a vitally important film. But films that win large audiences and continue to be viewed and discussed do, *ipso facto*, become important.

The meaning, or tendency of a movie is never absolute. Since film is polysemic, its meanings are multiple and fluid, and its intentional meanings are not the only, or necessarily the most important, ones. Viewers will see what they choose to see, whatever the director's purpose. Reception theory now favours the concept of an active audience as well as a divided one, making meanings from the text rather than hypnotically absorbing a single message. This more complex model allows scope for audience creativity, within the obvious limits of what verifiably appears on the screen.

Among reviewers and critics, *Easy Rider* is often regarded as a cultish freak show thrown up by the complications of its time. Pauline Kael has referred

audiences

Between two
worlds: George
takes a back seat,
his football helmet
and suit not quite
de rigueur for
a gonzo tripper

a film without a pronounced moral

in passing to its 'sentimental paranoia': a trendy, uncritical embrace of the countercultural lifestyle, an overstated fear of retribution. In David E. James's view it is unprogressive: 'finally reducible to and incorporable into the dominant ideological field'. To Chris Hugo *Easy Rider* is 'a reworking of old Hollywood traditions to suit contemporary notions of what was fashionable'. Sybil Delgaudio argues that it is 'self-defeating because it is self-conscious; by communicating extremes in terms of both message and style, the film denies the possibility of real alternatives, burying its values in the datedness of cultural faddism'.

The repeated downplaying of *Easy Rider* as a dated curiosity, like flared jeans or a peace sign, signals an unease running deeper than critical responses to a single movie. It is true that there are conservative elements, formally and thematically, in *Easy Rider*, above all in George Hanson's backward-looking rhetoric. It is also true that it offers no positive 'alternative' solutions; Billy and Wyatt are ignorant and indifferent about politics. And they are not brave or noble characters, just a pair of freewheeling losers. But the effect of all this is to give the film a curious near-objectivity. It has no sectarian axe to grind, despite its basic affinities. For the original audience it must have offered a sympathetic vacancy to be filled by the various wishes and dreams of those who, one way or another, felt the critical pressures of the national security state. As the 1960s' saying ran: 'If you're not paranoid you don't know what's going on.'

easy rider today

Easy Rider, still available as a full-price video, carries an 18 certificate, adults only. That puts it alongside films that have far more sex and violence (not to mention profanity – Billy and Wyatt are quite clean-spoken). A few seconds of violence, distilled from a context of much greater violence, plus some brief and fairly innocent nudity, can hardly explain the BBFC's decision. The most obvious reason for the classification is the movie's easygoing attitude to leisure drugs. It is not an amoral film, but it is a film without a pronounced moral. What is certain is that, while *Easy Rider's* sympathies are less facile than many critics have supposed, they do not favour those whose only method of protest or disagreement is a gun, and 'doing their own thing in their own time'

under Johnson and Nixon massive retaliation appeared to be United States government policy.

Neither side has a perfect case. The easy riders are hustlers and dropouts, buying the irresponsible detachment they confuse with freedom, and their hands are not quite clean. Their enemies are scared, parochial brutes with pinched mental horizons. The hippies, conducting a fragile experiment in alternative living, do not count as a third force. As a picture of America at the time, it is certainly 'ultra', but not wholly distorted.

The Vietnam War ended with victory for the NLF, the final rallying cry of the New Left. Two contradictory monuments in the heart of Washington remember the American dead. Nixon's own paranoia destroyed his presidency thanks to the scandal of Watergate (when in 1972 the Democratic National Committee offices in the Watergate complex in Washington were broken into, and President Nixon became involved in a cover-up). Reagan and Bush turned America to the right, and freely aired their contempt for peaceniks. Guns are still used to express differences and complaints. The sunshine of a general prosperity and the absence of war (what Nixon promised, in fact) hides social divisions. The mainstream film industry has grown more cautious, overreliant on blockbusters and protracted sequels, though innovation still squeezes in. Fans of *Easy Rider* post their artless tributes on the Net.

In the small but hyperactive world of Film Studies, an impressive database of analysis and opinion keeps cinema alive as a serious object of study and a rich source of pleasure. There, *Easy Rider*, though extensively namechecked, has few committed admirers, largely because the test of approval is often a film's adequately theorised challenge to the *status quo*, or failing that its underlying utopian vision. Billy's and Wyatt's quest is too vague and personal to qualify as utopian, and it ends in defeat and death. All the same, they are 'doing their own thing in their own time', not the most inspirational of mottoes, but never the worst.

bibliography

general film

Altman, Rick, *Film Genre*,
Routledge, 1981
  Detailed exploration of film genres

Bordwell, David, *Narration in the Fiction Film*, Routledge, 1985
  A detailed study of narrative theory and structures

– – – *The Classical Hollywood Cinema: Film Style & Mode of Production to 1960*, Routledge, 1985; pprbk 1995
  An authoritative study of cinema as institution, it covers film style and production

Bordwell, David & Thompson, Kristin, *Film Art*, McGraw-Hill, 4th edn, 1993
  An introduction to film aesthetics for the non-specialist

Branson, Gill & Stafford, Roy, *The Media Studies Handbook*, Routledge, 1996

Buckland, Warren, *Teach Yourself Film Studies*, Hodder & Stoughton, 1998
  Very accessible, it gives an overview of key areas in film studies

Cook, Pam (ed.), *The Cinema Book*, British Film Institute, 1994

Corrigan, Tim, *A Short Guide To Writing About Film*, HarperCollins, 1994
  What it says: a practical guide for students

Dyer, Richard, *Stars*, London BFI, 1979
  A good introduction to the star system

Easthope, Antony, *Classical Film Theory*, Longman, 1993
  A clear overview of recent writing about film theory

Hayward, Susan, *Key Concepts in Cinema Studies*, Routledge, 1996

Hill, & Gibson (eds), *The Oxford Guide to Film Studies*, Oxford, 1998
  Wide-ranging standard guide

Lapsley, Robert & Westlake, Michael, *Film Theory: An Introduction*, Manchester University Press, 1994

Maltby, Richard & Craven, Ian, *Hollywood Cinema*, Blackwell, 1995
  A comprehensive work on the Hollywood industry and its products

Nelmes, Jill (ed.), *Introduction to Film Studies*, Routledge, 1996
  Deals with several national cinemas and key concepts in film study

Nowell-Smith, Geoffrey (ed.), *The Oxford History of World Cinema*, Oxford, 1996
  Hugely detailed and wide-ranging with many features on 'stars'

Thomson, David, *A Biographical Dictionary of the Cinema*, Secker & Warburg, 1975
  Unashamedly driven by personal taste, but often stimulating

Truffaut, François, *Hitchcock*, New York, Simon & Schuster, 1966, rev.ed. Touchstone, 1985
  Landmark extended interview

Turner, Graham, *Film as Social Practice*, Routledge, 1993

Wollen, Peter, *Signs and Meaning in the Cinema*, New York, Viking 1972
  An important study in semiology

EASY RIDER

Readers should also explore the many relevant websites and journals. *Film Education* and *Sight and Sound* are standard reading.

Valuable websites include:

The Internet Movie Database at http://uk.imdb.com/

Screensite at http://www.tcf.ua.edu/screensite/contents.htm

The Media and Communications Site at the University of Aberystwyth at http://www.aber.ac.uk/~dgc/welcome.html

There are obviously many other university and studio websites which are worth exploring in relation to film studies.

easy rider

Adair, Gilbert, *Hollywood's Vietnam*, Heinemann, 1989
> Chapter 3 registers the 'absence' of Vietnam in *Easy Rider*

Andrew, Geoff, *Stranger than Paradise*, Prion, 1998
> A study of 'maverick film-makers in recent American cinema'

Biskind, Peter, *Easy Riders, Raging Bulls*, Bloomsbury, 1998
> Its narrative of the production set-up, shooting and editing of *Easy Rider* includes details of the quarrels and disagreements

Carson, L. M. Kit, 'Easy Rider: A Very American Thing', *Evergreen Review*, November 1969
> An interview with a wired Dennis Hopper after the opening of *Easy Rider*

Christensen, Terry, *Reel Politics*, Basil Blackwell, 1987
> The section on the 1960s oddly characterises Wyatt as 'a saint-like hippie leader' and notes that *Easy Rider* seems 'less political now than it did at the time'

Collier, Peter, *The Fondas*, Putnam, 1991
> A portrait of the acting dynasty, with background information on *Easy Rider*

Corman, Roger (with Jim Jerome), *How I Made a Hundred Movies in Hollywood and Never Lost a Dime*, Muller, 1990
> In Chapter 12 Corman gives his own view of the background to *Easy Rider*, including his regret at 'pulling out'

Davies, Philip & Neve, Brian (eds), *Cinema, Politics and Society in America*, Manchester University Press, 1981
> Though there is – surprisingly – no mention of *Easy Rider* in this collection, Eric Mottram's piece on cars in Hollywood movies is handily suggestive

Dick, Bernard F. (ed.), *Columbia Pictures*, University Press of Kentucky, Lexington, 1992
> Includes Sybil Delgaudio's essay on Columbia's 'trilogy of defeat', grouping *Easy Rider* with *Bob & Carol & Ted & Alice* (1969) and *The Big Chill* (1983)

Ehrenstein, David & Reed, Bill, *Rock on Film*, Virgin Books, 1982
> Primarily a checklist, but Chapter 7, 'Soundtrack Rock', is relevant

Farber – Schaefer

Farber, Manny, *Negative Space*,
Studio Vista, 1971
  Farber's original review of *Easy Rider* appears in the 'Clutter' section

Fonda, Peter, *Don't Tell Dad*,
Simon & Schuster, 1998
  Fonda's autobiography includes a detailed memoir of the origins and making of *Easy Rider*

Fonda, Peter, Hopper, Dennis & Southern, Terry,
Easy Rider, Signet, 1969
  The published script, edited by Nancy Hardin and Marilyn Schlossberg, with introductory essays and interviews. All direct quotations from the film in the text are from this version of the cutting continuity.

Hill, Lee, *Easy Rider*, BFI, 1996
  A lucid and sympathetic monograph, placing special stress on Terry Southern's contribution

Hillier, Jim, *The New Hollywood*,
Studio Vista, 1992
  Situates *Easy Rider* as a landmark film in the transition to New Hollywood

Izod, John, *Hollywood & the Box Office 1895–1986*, Macmillan 1988
  Chapters 12 and 13 cover the economic and industrial context of New Hollywood

Litwak, Mark, *Reel Power*,
Sidgwick & Jackson, 1986
  A fairly informal look at New Hollywood, with the youth market discussed in Chapter 6.

McCann, Graham, *Rebel Males*,
Hamish Hamilton, 1991
  McCann examines the stars who created rebel images in the 1950s.

McGilligan, Patrick,
'Stars Behind the Lens',
Take One, January 1979
  Includes a thumbnail account of Laszlo Kovács's work by a biographer of Jack Nicholson

Monaco, James,
American Film Now,
Plume, 1979
  Primarily on the 1970s, but the earlier chapters are useful for context

– – – *How to Read a Film*,
OUP, 1981
  One of the most accessible of Film Studies primers

Oldham, Gabriella, *First Cut*,
University of California Press, 1992
  Subtitled 'Conversations with Film Editors', it includes an interview with Donn Cambern

Pechter, William S.,
Twenty-four Times a Second: Films and Film-makers,
Harper & Row, 1971
  Pechter finds *Easy Rider* both 'mindless' and 'authentic'

Quart, Leonard & Auster, Albert,
American Film & Society Since 1945,
Macmillan, 1984
  A measured appraisal of *Easy Rider* in Chapter 4, 'The Sixties'

Sackett, Susan, *The Hollywood Reporter Book of Box Office Hits*,
Billboard Books, 1996
  The entry on *Easy Rider* quotes the production cost as $550,000 and the world grosses at $60,000,000

Schaefer, Dennis & Salvato, Larry,
Masters of Light,
University of California Press 1984
  Chapter 8 examines the work of Laszlo Kovács

Thompson, Peter,
Jack Nicholson, Birch Lane Press, 1997
   A tabloid-style biography, claiming
   105 joints were smoked during takes
   for the third camp-fire scene

Tischler, Barbara L. (ed.),
Sights on the Sixties,
Rutgers University Press, New
Brunswick, 1992
   Contains David Sanjek's essay
   'Apocalypse Then', critical of *Easy
   Rider*

Van Gelder, Peter,
Offscreen, Onscreen, Aurum 1990
   A light treatment – facts, anecdotes,
   review extracts – that plays down
   Terry Southern's contribution to *Easy
   Rider*

Williams, Mark, **Road Movies**,
Proteus Books, 1982
   Williams's choices verge on the
   indiscriminate, but the introductory
   material is worth reading

the sixties

Buckley, Jonathan and Ellingham,
Mark (eds), **Rock: The Rough Guide**,
Rough Guides, 1996
   An encyclopaedic reference source

Gitlin, Todd, **The Sixties:
Years of Hope, Days of Rage**,
Bantam Books, rev. ed., 1993
   A thoughtful and committed study of
   the time by a former SDS activist

Mairowitz, David Zane,
The Radical Soap Opera, Penguin, 1976
   Later chapters give a scathing account
   of the New Left

Morgan, Edward P., **The 60s
Experience**, Temple University Press,
Philadelphia, 1991
   Focuses on the play-off between
   idealism and pragmatism in the
   counterculture and the New Left

O'Neill, William L.,
Coming Apart, Times Books, 1971
   Published hard on the heels of 'The
   Sixties', it lacks the benefit of
   hindsight but projects the 'feel' of

the decade. Chapter 7 discusses
Easy Rider in the context of 'Two
Cultures'

Quart, Leonard & Auster, Albert,
How the War Was Remembered,
Praeger, 1988
   Part II touches on the submerged
   Vietnam dimension of *Easy Rider*

Stansill, Peter, & Mairowitz, David
Zane (eds), **BAMN**, Penguin, 1971
   A collection of 'Outlaw Manifestos
   and Ephemera 1965-70', many of
   them wildly gonzo

Thompson, Hunter S.,
Fear and Loathing in Las Vegas,
Warner Books, 1971
   A classic of the New Journalism,
   relating a drug-saturated trip to 'the
   heart of the American dream'

Wolfe, Tom, **The Electric Kool-Aid
Acid Test**, Bantam, 1969
   Wolfe's 'non-fiction novel' relates the
   activities of Ken Kesey and the Merry
   Pranksters

cinematic terms

AIP American International Pictures

auteurisme the 'authorship theory' of cinema, giving priority to the role of the director, whose personal style and vision is deemed to be the key factor. A director not accorded the status of auteur may be known as a metteur-en-scène

back story what has happened before the narrative starts. Early sequences giving the history of Billy and Wyatt were cut from the final print of *Easy Rider*, leaving the back story to be imagined

BBFC British Board of Film Censors

cinéma-vérité a style of film-making that tries to achieve an effect of realism and spontaneity by techniques such as the use of hand-held cameras and minimal editing of sound and image

classic Hollywood the mainstream American film industry and its products as it existed from approximately 1930 to 1960. See studio system, below

closure the impression of completeness and finality achieved at the end of a literary or filmic work

connotations in semiotics, the wider associations of a word or image, as opposed to 'denotation', the plain, literal meaning. 'Heart' *denotes* an organ of circulation; it *connotes* love, passion, morale, etc.

counterculture overlapping with the New Left, though not always political, the counterculture was a movement of revolt among mainly middle-class youth. Long hair was one of its symbolic badges; rock music and drugs signalled its iconoclastic energy

dénouement 'unravelling' – the disentangling of narrative strands in a work of fiction to provide a final resolution

diegetic from 'diegesis', meaning 'narrative'. Whatever is diegetic belongs within the narrative of a film. Superimposed music is non-diegetic The back story is pre-diegetic

dissolve screen syntax commonly used in classic Hollywood, in which one shot is gradually superimposed on another, signifying a time lapse. See fade

eclectic 'multiply sourced' – an eclectic work will draw on a variety of styles and ideas

existential a complex philosophical term, but in discussions of literature and film it commonly refers to the hero's efforts to bring meaning into an absurd world, or win freedom from the constraints of society, by personal choice and decisive, often extreme, action

fade the screen image is faded-out, usually to black, before the next image is faded in. It implies a longer time lapse than a dissolve

flash cut a very brief shot; in *Easy Rider* six-frame flash cuts appear as flash-forwards in the early camp-fire scenes and the brothel sequence

iconography the expressive pictorial motifs often associated with a genre. *Easy Rider* draws on the iconography of the Western

intertextuality a relationship between two or more art works that allows them to be read meaningfully in terms of one another

jump cut in film, an abrupt as opposed to a smooth transition, compressing time and/or space

Lévi-Strauss Claude Lévi-Strauss's concept of 'binary oppositions', originally designed to tease out the meaning of tribal or classical myths, has been widely employed to analyse narrative in film and literature

master shot sometimes 'establishing shot' or 'cover shot'. A master shot, usually a long shot, sets the scene

mimetic from 'mimesis', meaning the imitation of life, mimetic is applied to realistic art works

montage either just 'editing', or more commonly the rapid and forceful 'impact editing' first theorised by the Soviet film-maker Sergei Eisenstein

New Hollywood the American film industry as it has developed from the 1960s, following the break-up of the old studio system

points a percentage of the gross profits contractually due to a major participant (producer, director, star, etc.) in a film

polysemic 'having many meanings'. Cinema is an information-rich visual medium, in which meanings are multiple and subject to various 'readings'

preview system the preview system evolved in Hollywood as a way of test-marketing films. New movies were exhibited before general release to gauge the reaction of audiences, who filled in preview cards

Propp Vladimir Propp, in his *Morphology of the Folk Tale* (1928), identified a sequence of 'narrative functions' common to a sample of traditional Russian tales. Propp's method has subsequently been adapted to study narrative in modern and contemporary texts

reception reception studies, a growing concern of writers on film, consider how audiences 'receive' films, what meanings and impressions they take from them

scale working for scale means working for the minimum union rate. Costs were kept low on *Easy Rider* by adopting a union scale normally applied to television productions

semidocumentary a style that mimics the techniques of documentary (such as location shooting, a 'rough' or spontaneous look, improvised dialogue) to add to the realism of feature films

semiotic semiotics (or semiology) is the study of signs. In cinema the principal sign is the image (or 'iconic sign'). Analytically, the sign is divisible into the 'signifier' – the image itself – and the 'signified' – what it means

sleeper a sleeper is a surprise success – usually made for little money and not lavishly promoted

specific form the element that distinguishes a particular medium – in the case of cinema, moving photographic images

studio system classic Hollywood operated from a base of eight major studios: the 'Big Five' (MGM, Warner Bros, Paramount, Twentieth Century-Fox, RKO) and the 'Little Three' (Columbia, Universal-International, United Artists)

vertically integrated vertical integration meant that big studios owned the means of production, distribution and exhibition of films. Federal action under anti-trust laws, started before the Second World War and completed after it, dismantled the studios' vertically integrated structure

Zeitgeist 'the spirit of the age': a loose and often inadequate term, but one which suggests a relationship between art, ideas and their historical context

credits

production company
Raybert Productions (released through Columbia Pictures)

director
Dennis Hopper

producer
Peter Fonda

screenplay
Peter Fonda, Dennis Hopper, Terry Southern

cinematographer
Laszlo Kovacs

editor
Donn Cambern

art director
Jerry Kay

executive producer
Bert Schneider

associate producer
William L. Hayward

script supervisor
Joyce King

assistant editor
Stanley Siegel

cast
Wyatt – Peter Fonda
Billy – Dennis Hopper
George Hanson – Jack Nicholson
Jesus – Antonio Mendoza
Connection – Phil Spector
Rancher – Warren Finnerty
Stranger on Highway – Luke Askew
Lisa – Luana Anders
Karen – Karen Black
Mary – Toni Basil

songs
Steppenwolf, 'Pusher'

Steppenwolf, 'Born To Be Wild'

The Byrds, 'Wasn't Born To Follow'

The Band, 'The Weight'

The Holy Modal Rounders, 'If You Want To Be A Bird'

Fraternity Of Men, 'Don't Bogart Me'

The Jimi Hendrix Experience, 'If Six Was Nine'

Little Eva, 'Let's Turkey Trot'

The Electric Prunes, 'Kyrie Eleison'

The Electric Flag, 'Flash, Bang, Pow'

Roger McGuin, 'It's All Right, Ma (I'm Only Bleeding)'

Roger McGuinn, 'The Ballad Of Easy Rider'

Other titles in the series

Other titles available in the York Film Notes series:

Title	ISBN
8½	0582 40488 6
A Bout de Souffle	0582 43182 4
Apocalypse Now	0582 43183 2
Battleship Potemkin	0582 40490 8
Blade Runner	0582 43198 0
Casablanca	0582 43201 4
Chinatown	0582 43199 9
Citizen Kane	0582 40493 2
Das Cabinet des Dr Caligari	0582 40494 0
Double Indemnity	0582 43196 4
Dracula	0582 43197 2
Easy Rider	0582 43195 6
Fargo	0582 43193 X
La Haine	0582 43194 8
Lawrence of Arabia	0582 43192 1
Psycho	0582 43191 3
Pulp Fiction	0582 40510 6
Romeo and Juliet	0582 43189 1
Some Like It Hot	0582 40503 3
Stagecoach	0582 43187 5
Taxi Driver	0582 40506 8
Terminator	0582 43186 7
The Full Monty	0582 43181 6
The Godfather	0582 43188 3
The Piano	0582 43190 5
The Searchers	0582 40510 6
The Third Man	0582 40511 4
Thelma and Louise	0582 43184 0
Unforgiven	0582 43185 9

Also from York Notes

Also available in the **York Notes** range:

York Notes
The ultimate literature guides for GCSE students (or equivalent levels)

York Notes Advanced
Literature guides for A-level and undergraduate students (or equivalent levels)

York Personal Tutors
Personal Tutoring on essential GCSE English and Maths topics

Available from good bookshops.
For full details, please visit our website at www.longman-yorknotes.com

EASY RIDER

.